Microsoft Azure Security Infrastructure

Yuri Diogenes
Dr. Thomas W. Shinder
Debra Littlejohn Shinder

PUBLISHED BY
Microsoft Press
A division of Microsoft Corporation
One Microsoft Way
Redmond, Washington 98052-6399

Library of Congress Control Number: 2016938684
ISBN: 978-1-5093-0357-1

Printed and bound in the United States of America.

1 16

Microsoft Press books are available through booksellers and distributors worldwide. If you need support related to this book, email Microsoft Press Support at mspinput@microsoft.com. Please tell us what you think of this book at http://aka.ms/tellpress.

This book is provided "as-is" and expresses the author's views and opinions. The views, opinions and information expressed in this book, including URL and other Internet website references, may change without notice.

Some examples depicted herein are provided for illustration only and are fictitious. No real association or connection is intended or should be inferred.

Microsoft and the trademarks listed at http://www.microsoft.com on the "Trademarks" webpage are trademarks of the Microsoft group of companies. All other marks are property of their respective owners.

Acquisitions and Developmental Editor: Karen Szall
Editorial Production: Online Training Solutions, Inc. (OTSI)
Technical Reviewer: Mike Toot; technical review services provided by Content Master, a member of CM Group, Ltd.
Copyeditor: Jaime Odell (OTSI)
Indexer: Susie Carr (OTSI)
Cover: Twist Creative • Seattle

Contents

What do you think of this book? We want to hear from you!

Microsoft is interested in hearing your feedback so we can improve our books and learning resources for you. To participate in a brief survey, please visit:

http://aka.ms/tellpress

What do you think of this book? We want to hear from you!

Microsoft is interested in hearing your feedback so we can improve our books and learning resources for you. To participate in a brief survey, please visit:

http://aka.ms/tellpress

Foreword

Security is a critical requirement of any software system, but in today's world of diverse, skilled, and motivated attackers, it's more important than ever. In the past, security efforts focused on creating the strongest possible wall to keep attackers out. Security professionals considered the Internet hostile, and treated their own company or organization's systems as the trusted inner core, making relatively modest investments in segregating different environments and visibility into the interactions between different components. Now, the security world has adopted an "assume breach" mindset that treats perimeter networks as just one aspect of the protective pillar in a three-pillar approach that also includes detection and response. Attackers can and will penetrate the strongest defenses, and they can enter the network from inside. The perimeter is gone, and security architectures and investments are continuing to shift to address the new reality.

At the same time that the changing threat landscape is reshaping the approach to security, people have embarked on shifting their compute and data from infrastructure they deploy and maintain to that hosted by hyper-scale public cloud service providers. Infrastructure as a service (IaaS) and platform as a service (PaaS) dramatically increase agility by offering on-demand, elastic, and scalable compute and data. IT professionals and application developers can focus on their core mission: delivering compliant, standardized services to their organizations in the case of the former, and quickly delivering new features and functionality to the business and its customers in the latter.

You're reading this book because your organization is considering or has begun adopting public cloud services. You likely have already recognized that the introduction of the cloud provider into your network architecture creates new challenges. Whereas in your on-premises networks you use firewall appliances and physical routing rules to segregate environments and monitor traffic, the public cloud exposes virtualized networks, software load balancers, and application gateways, along with abstractions such as network security groups, that take their place. In some cases, the cloud offers services that give you insight and control that's either impossible or hard to achieve on-premises, making it easier to deliver high levels of security. The terminology, tools, and techniques are different, and creating secure and resilient "assume breach" cloud and hybrid systems requires a deep understanding of what's available and how to best apply it.

This book will serve as your trusted guide as you create and move applications and data to Microsoft Azure. The first step to implementing security in the cloud is knowing what the platform does for you and what your responsibility is, which is different depending on whether you're using IaaS, PaaS, or finished software services like Microsoft Office 365. After describing the differences, Yuri, Tom and Deb then move on to cover everything from identity and access control, to how to create a cloud network for your virtual machines, to how to more securely connect the cloud to your on-premises networks. You'll also learn how to manage keys and certificates, how to encrypt data at rest and in transit, how the Azure Security Center vulnerability and threat reporting can show you where you can improve security, and how Azure Security Center even walks you through doing so. Finally, the cloud and Internet of Things (IoT) are synergistic technologies, and if you're building an IoT solution on Azure, you'll benefit from the practical advice and tips on pitfalls to avoid.

The advent of the cloud requires new skills and knowledge, and those skills and knowledge will mean not only that you can more effectively help your organization use the cloud, but that you won't be left behind in this technology shift. With this book, you'll be confident that you have an end-to-end view of considerations, options, and even details of how to deploy and manage more secure applications on Azure.

— MARK RUSSINOVICH
CTO, Microsoft Azure
July 2016

Introduction

Regardless of your title, if you're responsible for designing, configuring, implementing, or managing secure solutions in Microsoft Azure, then this book is for you. If you're a member of a team responsible for architecting, designing, implementing, and managing secure solutions in Azure, this book will help you understand what your team needs to know. If you're responsible for managing a consulting firm that is implementing secure solutions in Azure, you should read this book. And if you just want to learn more about Azure security to improve your skill set or aid in a job search, this book will help you understand Azure security services and technologies and how to best use them to better secure an Azure environment.

This book includes conceptual information, design considerations, deployment scenarios, best practices, technology surveys, and how-to content, which will provide you with a wide view of what Azure has to offer in terms of security. In addition, numerous links to supplemental information are included to speed your learning process.

This book is a "must read" for anyone who is interested in Azure security. The authors assume that you have a working knowledge of cloud computing basics and core Azure concepts, but they do not expect you to be an Azure or PowerShell expert. They assume that you have enterprise IT experience and are comfortable in a datacenter. If you need more detailed information about how to implement the Azure security services and technologies discussed in this book, be sure to check out the references to excellent how-to articles on *Azure.com*.

Acknowledgments

The authors would like to thank Karen Szall and the entire Microsoft Press team for their support in this project, Mark Russinovich for writing the foreword of this book, and also other Microsoft colleagues that contributed by reviewing this book: Rakesh Narayan, Eric Jarvi, Meir Mendelovich, Daniel Alon, Sarah Fender, Ben Nick, Russ McRee, Jim Molini, Jon Ormond, Devendra Tiwari, Nasos Kladakis, and Arjmand Samuel.

Yuri: I would also like to thank my wife and daughters for their endless support and understanding, my great God for giving me strength and guiding my path, my friends and coauthors Tom and Deb Shinder, my manager Sonia Wadhwa for her support in my role, and last but not least, to my parents for working hard to give me education, which is the foundation that I use every day to keep moving forward in my career.

Tom and Deb Shinder: Writing—even with coauthors—is in some ways an isolated task. You sit down at the keyboard (or in today's high tech, alternative input environment, dictate into your phone or even scribble onto your tablet screen) alone, and let the words flow from your mind to the document. However, the formation of those words and sentences and paragraphs and the fine-tuning of them through the editing and proofing process are based on the input of many, many other people.

Because there are far too many colleagues, experts, and friends and family who had a role in making it possible for this book to come into being, we aren't going to even attempt to name them all here. You know who you are. From the family members who patiently waited while we finished up a chapter, delaying dinner, to the myriad of Azure professionals both within and outside of Microsoft, to the folks at Microsoft Press whose publishing expertise helped shape this collection of writing from three different authors with very different writing styles into a coherent whole, and most of all, to those who asked for and will read and (we hope) benefit from this book: we thank you.

Free ebooks from Microsoft Press

From technical overviews to in-depth information on special topics, the free ebooks from Microsoft Press cover a wide range of topics. These ebooks are available in PDF, EPUB, and Mobi for Kindle formats, ready for you to download at:

http://aka.ms/mspressfree

Check back often to see what is new!

Errata, updates, & book support

We've made every effort to ensure the accuracy of this book and its companion content. You can access updates to this book—in the form of a list of submitted errata and their related corrections—at:

http://aka.ms/AzSecInfra/errata

If you discover an error that is not already listed, please submit it to us from the same page.

If you need additional support, email Microsoft Press Book Support at:

mspinput@microsoft.com

Please note that product support for Microsoft software and hardware is not offered through the previous addresses. For help with Microsoft software or hardware, go to:

http://support.microsoft.com

We want to hear from you

At Microsoft Press, your satisfaction is our top priority, and your feedback our most valuable asset. Please tell us what you think of this book at:

http://aka.ms/tellpress

The survey is short, and we read every one of your comments and ideas. Thanks in advance for your input!

Stay in touch

Let's keep the conversation going! We're on Twitter at:

http://twitter.com/MicrosoftPress

## CHAPTER 1

Cloud security

Before you dive into the details about Microsoft Azure security infrastructure—the main subject of this book—it is important to have clear expectations regarding cloud security. To understand what makes Azure a trusted cloud platform for customers, you must first understand the essential considerations regarding security in the cloud. Security in the cloud is a partnership between you and the service provider. This chapter explains key characteristics that will enable you to understand the boundaries, responsibilities, and expectations that will help you embrace cloud computing as a trusted platform for your business.

Cloud security considerations

Before adopting cloud computing to its fullest, organizations must first understand the security considerations that are inherent in this computing model. It is very important to understand these considerations in the beginning of the planning process. Lack of awareness regarding cloud security considerations can directly impact a successful cloud computing adoption and compromise the entire project.

When planning for cloud adoption, consider the following areas for cloud security:

- Compliance
- Risk management
- Identity and access management
- Operational security
- Endpoint protection
- Data protection

Each of these areas must be considered, with some areas explored in more depth than others, depending on the type of business that you are dealing with. For example, a health care provider might focus on different areas than a manufacturing company focuses on. The sections that follow describe each of these areas.

Compliance

When organizations migrate to the cloud, they need to retain their own compliance obligations. These obligations can be dictated by internal or external regulations, such as industry standards that they need to comply with to support their business model. Cloud providers must be able to assist customers to meet their compliance requirements via cloud adoption. In many cases, cloud service providers will become part of the customer's chain of compliance.

To enable customers to meet their compliance needs, Microsoft uses three major practices, which are:

- Compliance foundation
    - Trustworthy technology
    - Compliance process investment
    - Third-party certification
- Assistance for customers to meet their compliance needs
    - Transparency
    - Choice
    - Flexibility
- Partnership with industry leaders
    - Development of standard frameworks
    - Engagement with lawmakers and regulators

Consider working closely with your cloud provider to identify your organization's compliance needs and verify how the cloud provider can fulfill your requirements. It is also important to verify whether the cloud service provider has a proven record of delivering the most secure, reliable cloud services while keeping customers' data as private and secure as possible.

> **MORE INFO**   For more information about the Microsoft approach to compliance, go to *blogs.microsoft.com/on-the-issues/2016/04/07 /new-resources-microsoft-support-customer-privacy-cloud-compliance*.

Risk management

When customers adopt cloud computing, it is imperative that they are able to trust the location used by the cloud service provider. Cloud service providers should have policies and programs that are used to manage online security risks. In a cloud environment, risk management must be adapted to how dynamic the environment is.

Microsoft uses mature processes based on long-term experience delivering services on the web for managing these new risks. As part of the risk management process, cloud service providers should perform the following tasks:

- Identify threats and vulnerabilities to the environment.
- Calculate risk.
- Report risks across the cloud environment.
- Address risks based on impact assessment and the associated business case.
- Test potential remediation effectiveness and calculate residual risk.
- Manage risks on an ongoing basis.

Customers should work closely with cloud service providers and demand full process transparency to be able to understand risk decisions, how this will vary according to the data sensitivity, and the level of protection required by the organization.

Identity and access management

Nowadays, when users are working on different devices from any location and accessing apps across different cloud services, it is critical to keep the user's identity secure. With cloud adoption, identity becomes the new perimeter. Identity is the control pane for your entire infrastructure, regardless of the location: on-premises or in the cloud. You use identity to control access to any services from any device, and you use it to get visibility and insights into how your data is being used.

Organizations planning to adopt cloud computing must be aware of the identity and access management methods available and how these methods integrate with their current on-premises infrastructure. Some key considerations for identity and access management are:

- Identity provisioning
    - Identity provisioning requirements can vary according to the cloud computing model: software as a service (SaaS), platform as a service (PaaS), or infrastructure as a service (IaaS).
    - Evaluate how to more securely automate the identity provisioning by using the current on-premises infrastructure.
- Federation
    - Evaluate the methods available and how to integrate these methods with the current on-premises infrastructure.
- Single sign-on (SSO)
    - Evaluate the organization's requirement for SSO and how to integrate it with current apps.
- Profile management
    - Evaluate cloud service provider options and how these options map with the organization's requirement.
- Access control
    - Evaluate cloud service provider options to control data access.
    - Enforce Role-Based Access Control (RBAC).

Operational security

Organizations that are migrating to the cloud should also modify their internal processes adequately to map to the cloud. These processes include security monitoring, auditing, incident response, and forensics. The cloud platform must enable IT administrators to monitor services in real time to observe health conditions of these services and provide capabilities to quickly restore services that were interrupted.

You should ensure that deployed services are operated, maintained, and supported in accordance with a service level agreement (SLA) established with the cloud service provider and agreed to by the organization. The following list provides additional considerations for operational security in the cloud:

- Incorporate organizational learning throughout the process.
- Adopt industry standards and practices for operations, such as National Institute of Standards and Technology (NIST) SP 800-53.[1]
- Use a security information management approach in line with industry standards, such as NIST SP 800-61.[2]
- Use the cloud service provider's threat intelligence.
- Continuously update controls and mitigations to enhance the operation's security.

Endpoint protection

Cloud security is not only about how secure the cloud service provider infrastructure is. Later in this chapter, you will learn more about shared responsibility, and one of the items that organizations are responsible for when adopting cloud computing is to keep their endpoint secure. Organizations should consider increasing their endpoint security when adopting cloud computing, because these endpoints will be exposed to more external connections and will be accessing more apps that could be living in different cloud providers.

Users are the main target of the attacks, and endpoints are the primary objects that are used by users to consume data. The endpoint can be the user's workstation, smartphone, or any device that can be used to access cloud resources. Attackers know that the end user is the weakest link in the security chain, and they will continue to invest in social engineering techniques, such as phishing email, to entice users to perform an action that can compromise the endpoint. Consider the following security best practices when planning for endpoint protection in your cloud security strategy:

- Keep endpoint software up to date.
- Use automatic deployment to deliver definition updates to endpoints.
- Control access to the download location for software updates.
- Ensure that end users do not have local administrative privileges.
- Use the principle of least privileges and role-based administration to grant permissions to users.
- Monitor endpoint alerts promptly.

> **IMPORTANT** Securing privileged access is a critical step to establishing security assurances for business. You can read about Privileged Access Workstations (PAWs) at *aka.ms/cyberpaw* and learn more about the Microsoft methodology to protect high-value assets.

---

[1] For more information about this standard, go to *nvlpubs.nist.gov/nistpubs/SpecialPublications/NIST.SP.800-53r4.pdf*.
[2] For more information about this standard, go to *nvlpubs.nist.gov/nistpubs/SpecialPublications/NIST.SP.800-61r2.pdf*.

Data protection

When the subject is cloud security, the ultimate goal when migrating to the cloud is to ensure that the data is secure no matter where this data is located. The data goes through different stages; the stage depends on where the data will be located at a certain point in time. Figure 1-1 illustrates these stages.

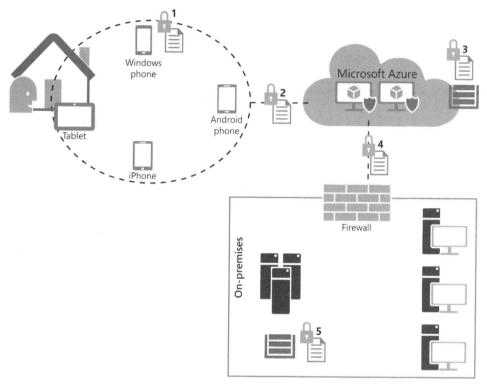

FIGURE 1-1 Different data stages by location

In this flow, the stages are:

1. **Data at rest in the user's device** In this case, the data is located at the endpoint, which can be any device. You should always enforce data encryption at rest for company-owned devices and user-owned devices (bring your own device [BYOD] scenarios).

2. **Data in transit from the user's device to the cloud** When data leaves the user's device, you should ensure that the data itself is still protected. Many technologies, such as Azure Rights Management, can encrypt the data regardless of the location. It is also imperative to ensure that the transport channel is encrypted; therefore, the use of Transport Layer Security (TLS) to transfer the data should always be enforced.

3. **Data at rest in the cloud provider's datacenter**   When the data arrives in the cloud provider's servers, their storage infrastructure should ensure redundancy and protection. Make sure you understand how your cloud service provider performs data encryption at rest, who is responsible for managing the keys, and how data redundancy is performed.

4. **Data in transit from the cloud to on-premises**   In this case, the same recommendations specified in stage 2 are applicable. Enforce data encryption on the file itself and encrypt the transport layer.

5. **Data at rest on-premises**   Customers are responsible for keeping their on-premises data secure. Data encryption at rest at the organization's datacenter is a critical step to accomplish that. Ensure that you have the correct infrastructure to enable encryption, data redundancy, and key management.

Cloud security considerations

Moving to the cloud requires different thinking. Scale, speed, and architecture mean that we must treat cloud-based services differently than local virtual machines (VMs) or time-shared mainframes. Here are a few of the topics that require special thought when you work with a cloud service provider like Azure.

Well-organized cloud services add or remove machines from the inventory in minutes or hours. Many can handle traffic spikes of more than 1,000 percent within a single day. Due to the rapid pace of development, daily or weekly code changes are normal, and testing must occur by using production services, but not sensitive production data.

Any organization moving to the cloud must establish a trust relationship with a cloud service provider and must use all of the tools available to define and enforce the negotiated requirements of that relationship.

I tell friends that in the 1990s, if I needed a dozen servers for a new project, it would take four to six months to forecast, order, deliver, rack, network, configure, and deploy those servers before the team could begin testing the production service. Today, in Azure, I can do the same thing in 30 minutes, from my phone.

Jim Molini
Senior Program Manager, C+E Security

Shared responsibility

In a traditional datacenter, the IT organization is responsible for the entire infrastructure. This is how on-premises computing has worked from the beginning of modern client/server computing (and even before that, in the mainframe era). If something was wrong with the network, storage, or compute infrastructure, the IT organization was responsible for finding out what the problem was, and fixing it.

The same went for the security organization. The security organization worked with the IT organization as a whole to ensure that all components of the IT infrastructure were secure. The corporate security organization set requirements, rationalized those requirements with the corporate IT organization, and then defined controls that could be implemented by the IT infrastructure and operations staff. The security organization also defined compliance requirements and was responsible for auditing the infrastructure to make sure that those requirements were met on an ongoing basis.

All of this is still true for the on-premises datacenter. However, with the introduction of public cloud computing, the IT and security organizations have a new partner—the cloud service provider. The cloud service provider has its own IT infrastructure and is responsible for the security requirements and controls implemented on that infrastructure.

This means you need to not only be aware of and define your own security requirements, you need to also be able to have enough visibility into the security infrastructure and operations of your cloud service provider. The extent to which you need to do this depends on the *cloud security model* your company is using on the cloud service provider's infrastructure.

Cloud computing

This section provides a quick review of cloud computing so you have a common understanding of what cloud computing is and what it is not. This will help you understand how cloud security works in the cloud and how it is the same in most respects, and different in some key areas, from traditional datacenter computing.

NIST definition of cloud computing

The term "cloud computing" had been used for some time without a formal definition. Of course, for those who have been in the industry for a while, "cloud" represents the Internet. And for some people, that was what cloud computing was about: services delivered over the Internet.

Some commentators used the term *utility computing* to convey the idea that not only are services delivered over the Internet, but that service delivery would take on a "utility" model. A utility model is one where a core set of capabilities is delivered to anyone who wants to "consume" those capabilities; the consumers are charged based on how much they use. This is similar to consumer utilities such as electricity and gas.

At this time, most countries/regions around the world and the companies within them accept the NIST definition of cloud computing to be the most reliable and actionable definition of cloud computing. NIST is the United States National Institute of Standards and Technology.

A major advance in understanding cloud computing came from NIST in the form of its "five essential characteristics" of cloud computing and the definition of cloud service models and cloud deployment models.

Figure 1-2 depicts the five essential characteristics, the cloud service models, and the cloud deployment models.

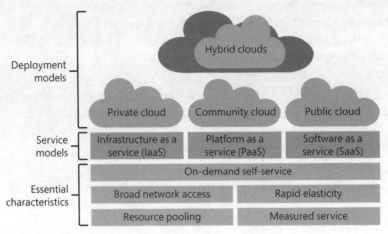

FIGURE 1-2 NIST definition of cloud computing

Cloud computing characteristics

NIST defines the following five essential characteristics of cloud computing:

- **On-demand self-service**   This refers to the cloud capability of enabling consumers of the cloud service to requisition required resources without needing to go through a process that requires user interaction. For example, users can use an online form to request and receive anything they need from the cloud service provider.

- **Broad network access**   This relates to the cloud capability of resources contained in the cloud to be available from virtually any location, and from almost any type of device in the world. It's important to point out that while broad network access is part of the definition of cloud computing, and the enabling of broad network access is key to successful cloud deployments, this does *not* mean that access is always granted. As you will learn as you proceed through this book, access control is a critical component of any cloud-based solution.

- **Rapid elasticity**   This provides consumers of a cloud service the ability to rapidly obtain cloud resources when they need them and then release those resources back into the cloud's shared pool of resources when they are no longer required. Cloud architectures offer elasticity of resources to consumers of the cloud service. From the tenant's perspective, the cloud offers an unlimited pool of resources. If the consumer of the cloud service anticipates a burst in demand for their service, the client can request more resources from the cloud to ensure that the service is capable of meeting that demand. The "perception of infinite capacity" is a key principle behind that of rapid elasticity.

- **Resource pooling** This is about having all consumers of a cloud service use the same pool of resources. All users of the cloud environment use the same servers, network, and storage; that resource pool is dynamically partitioned so that one customer cannot access any other customer's data, applications, and virtual machines. As explained later in this chapter, isolation at all levels is critical to the success of any cloud infrastructure because of the requirement for resource pooling.

- **Measured service** This means that consumers of the cloud service only pay for what they consume. This is very similar to a utility model where you only pay for what you use. For example, you only pay for the amount of electricity, water, or gas you use (although there might be some kind of "base" you have to pay to access the service). Measured service also means that the cloud service provider needs to be transparent in terms of providing consumers of the cloud service information about usage so that consumers can audit their usage to make predictions about future needs and costs.

Cloud service models

According to the NIST definition of cloud computing, there are three service models and four deployment models. The service model defines what level of service out of the entire solution stack the cloud service provider provides for its customers. The deployment models define how and to whom those services are delivered.

The cloud services models are:

- **Infrastructure as a service (IaaS)** This provides the core physical, processing, networking, and storage infrastructure. This infrastructure is owned and operated by the cloud service provider. The cloud service provider is responsible for maintaining the up-time and performance of this infrastructure. It is also responsible for the security of these components. In contrast to on-premises computing, with IaaS, you are not responsible for these core infrastructure aspects of any solution you put into a cloud service provider partner's cloud infrastructure.

- **Platform as a service (PaaS)** This provides everything you get with infrastructure as a service, but adds to it the development platform components. The cloud service provider is now responsible not only for the infrastructure, but also the operating system (or components that provide capabilities similar to an operating system), and the runtime environment (such as a web server platform) required to deliver customer-developed applications. The security of these operating systems and their equivalents, in addition to the runtime environment, is the responsibility of the cloud service provider and not the customer.

- **Software as a service (SaaS)** For this, which is sometimes referred to as "finished services," the cloud service provider is responsible for the entire infrastructure and platform. It is also responsible for the application environment. Software as a service provides customers with a complete application similar to those traditionally run on-premises, such as Microsoft Exchange Server email or Microsoft SharePoint collaboration. The cloud service provider is responsible for secure deployment and management of the application.

Cloud deployment models

NIST defines four deployment models:

- **Public cloud**   This deployment model is designed so that multiple customers from any place in the world can use a shared infrastructure. All customers in a public cloud share the same hardware—the same servers, the same network, and the same storage. Of course, all of these physical infrastructure components are deployed and managed at cloud scale. As explained later, the key in making sure that public cloud computing is successful is strong isolation—the ability to isolate one customer's assets from another customer's assets at all levels of the stack is the number one job responsibility of all public cloud service providers.

- **Private cloud**   This deployment model is a cloud environment hosted by the IT organization. A private cloud is not the same as a traditional on-premises datacenter (although the term is often misused in that way). In contrast to a traditional on-premises datacenter, a private cloud is able to deliver on all five of the essential characteristics of cloud computing as defined by NIST and as discussed previously. Private cloud is also concerned with isolation, although perhaps to a lesser extent than public cloud; that would depend on the use case scenario and the level of trust and security zoning that an organization has in place, and how much they want to reflect that into their cloud environment.

    The difference between public cloud and private cloud is that the organization owns all aspects of the private cloud and there are no dependencies or relationships with external entities.

- **Hybrid cloud**   This deployment model is a combination of a public cloud and a private cloud, in most cases. It is possible to have other types of hybrid clouds, such as a public cloud to a community cloud, or even two different public clouds. In the typical hybrid cloud deployment, components of a solution are placed in both the public cloud and the private cloud.

    For example, a three-tier application has a web front end, an application logic middle tier, and a database back end. In a hybrid cloud deployment, the front-end web servers and the application logic servers would be in the public cloud, and the database back end would be on-premises. In most cases, the on-premises network is connected to the public cloud via a cross-premises connection, such as a site-to-site virtual private network (VPN) or dedicated wide-area network (WAN) link.

- **Community cloud**   This deployment model is a variation of a public cloud, but in the case of community cloud, the public cloud environment is not open to all potential users. Instead, community cloud infrastructures are dedicated to a particular community, such as local, state, or federal government.

Distributed responsibility in public cloud computing

Now that you have an understanding of cloud computing, take a look at how it influences who is responsible for security. Figure 1-3 provides a general overview of who is responsible for various aspects of a solution that is deployed by using various deployment models.

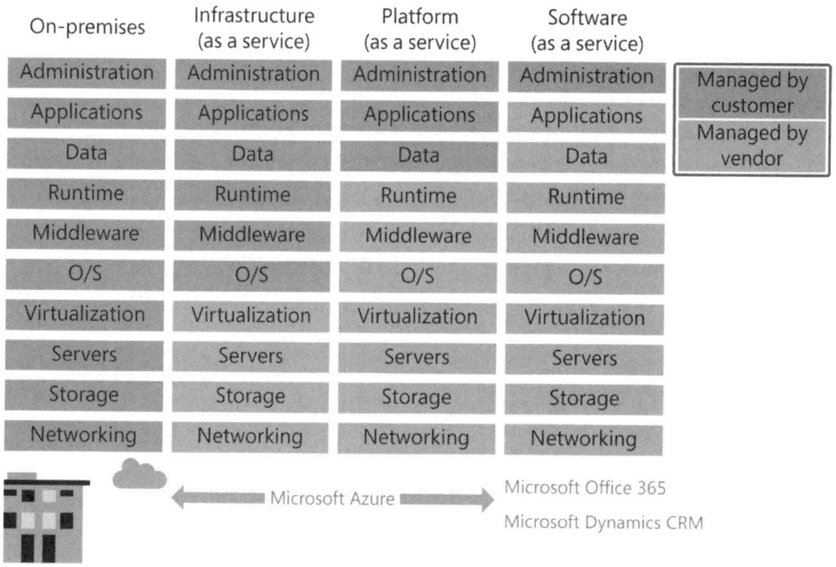

On-premises	Infrastructure (as a service)	Platform (as a service)	Software (as a service)	
Administration	Administration	Administration	Administration	Managed by customer
Applications	Applications	Applications	Applications	Managed by vendor
Data	Data	Data	Data	
Runtime	Runtime	Runtime	Runtime	
Middleware	Middleware	Middleware	Middleware	
O/S	O/S	O/S	O/S	
Virtualization	Virtualization	Virtualization	Virtualization	
Servers	Servers	Servers	Servers	
Storage	Storage	Storage	Storage	
Networking	Networking	Networking	Networking	

Microsoft Azure

Microsoft Office 365
Microsoft Dynamics CRM

FIGURE 1-3 Cloud services and responsibilities

This distribution of responsibility is one of the key security differences between traditional datacenter computing and on-premises computing.

Moving from left to right in the figure, you can see that for on-premises solutions, the entire responsibility for security belongs to the IT organization and company that owns the infrastructure. This is the pre-cloud computing approach to security, which you're most likely familiar with.

For infrastructure as a service, the cloud service provider becomes responsible for some of the security. Because infrastructure as a service is designed to provide you with core storage, networking, physical servers, and a virtualization platform, the responsibility for securing these levels of the stack belongs to the cloud service provider. As you move up the stack, above the components for which the cloud service provider is responsible, the responsibility for securing those components belongs to you.

With platform as a service, even more levels of the stack are managed by the cloud service provider, so there the cloud service provider is responsible for securing those additional levels and you have less to secure.

Finally, as you move to software as a service, the cloud service provider is responsible for managing all levels of the solution stack except for administrative tasks such as granting your users access to the service. With that said, most finished services have some controls for which you're responsible.

For example, Microsoft Office 365 provides you with email services, and Microsoft is responsible for making sure that the messaging environment is as secure as possible and all possible controls that Microsoft has access to are configured in a secure fashion. There are still some security controls that are made available to you, such as email encryption, attachment filtering, and others that you can deploy or not deploy. Therefore, even though with SaaS the cloud service provider is responsible for securing the entire stack, the cloud service provider is not responsible for enabling or disabling additional data controls to which only the customer has access.

Understanding the division of responsibility based on the cloud service deployment model is more than just an academic exercise. So, if you didn't understand what was covered here, read it over again. When you adopt a public cloud service provider and decide what applications you want to put into the cloud, you'll need to know how to map what you're responsible for and what your cloud service provider is responsible for, and then define your requirements and come up with your designs based on this understanding.

Assume breach and isolation

As previously mentioned, one of the most significant differences between traditional datacenter security and cloud security is the new distribution of the responsibility model based on what cloud deployment model you use.

Cloud computing security significantly differs from traditional datacenter security in two other major areas: assume breach and isolation, which are described in this section.

For the last several decades, the vast majority of time, effort, and money has been behind stopping something "bad" from happening. Some actions taken include the following:

- Deploying antivirus software
- Deploying antimalware
- Hardening operating systems
- Creating perimeter network segments and network security zones
- Instantiating data leakage protection
- Requiring complex passwords and passphrases
- Requiring multifactor authentication
- Encrypting file systems, disks, and individual documents
- Updating operating systems
- Scanning ports and testing pens
- Preventing distributed denial of service (DDoS) attacks
- Securing code development by using the Microsoft Security Development Lifecycle
- Scanning for vulnerabilities

We've done all those things. And we've done them again as the technologies in these areas have improved. We bought the best, deployed with secure best practices, and managed the heck out of our security solutions.

What happened?

Read your daily newspaper or news site. You know what happened: almost daily breaches of the largest companies and governments in the world. All these corporate and government entities did what they could do from a greater or lesser extent to prevent breach. They spent the money, they deployed the products, they met compliance requirements and passed the audits.

And they were breached.

Now that's not to say that you should *stop* doing all these things to prevent breach. Imagine the exponential increase in security incidents if people weren't doing all of these things! Breach prevention makes it harder for someone to compromise your systems. It slows attackers down, and in many cases, stops them. But for the determined opponent, the one who stands to make thousands, hundreds of thousands, millions, or tens of millions from breaching your systems, traditional prevent breach processes and technologies are not enough.

Microsoft recognizes that preventing breach is not enough. That doesn't mean we've "given up" or "thrown in the towel" when it comes to breach prevention. We continue to use all the traditional breach prevention processes and technologies, and we'll continue to use them as new processes are invented. However, in addition to those, we realize that we have to do more.

That "more" is encompassed by a philosophy of "assume breach." An assume breach mentality means that people hope that they will never be breached. However, we know that hope is a poor strategy. Therefore, we assume that we are about to be breached, or have already been breached, and we have people, processes, and technology that help us find out when the breach occurred as early as possible, and then we eject the attacker with the goal being to limit expansion of the breach as much as possible.

We use the assume breach approach to help us understand how attackers gain access to the system and then develop methods that enable us to catch the attacker as soon as possible after the breach takes place. Because attackers typically enter a system via a low value target, if we can detect quickly when the target has been compromised, we can block the attacker from expanding outward from the low value asset to higher value assets; these high value assets are the attacker's ultimate target.

How does Microsoft determine when an attack occurred? One very effective method we use is Red Teaming, or Red/Blue team simulations. In these exercises, the Red Team takes on the role of the attacker and the Blue Team takes on the role of defender. The teams define the parameters of the exercise and then for the time duration for which the exercise is agreed upon, the Red Team tries to attack the Azure infrastructure and the Blue Team tries to discover what the Red Team has done and then attempts to block the Red Team from compromising additional systems (if indeed the Red Team was able to compromise any systems).

At the end of the exercise, the Red and Blue teams discuss what happened, how the Red Team might have gotten in, and how the Blue team discovered and ejected the Red Team. Then they suggest new technologies and operational procedures that will make it easier and faster to discover compromise.

In addition to these exercises, we have an active bug bounty program, use the latest in security monitoring and response, and take advantage of the latest threat intelligence, which is shared among all the major cloud service providers.

"Assume breach" does not mean "assume failure"

We adopt the "assume breach" concept as a mental guideline to use when designing security services and not as resignation to failure. In a "prevent breach" environment, we'd often build strong perimeter controls, but pay less attention to compartmentalization inside the organization. Remember the old concept of hard outside and soft, chewy center? Nevertheless, the ongoing threat from bad actors requires better thinking.

Using the assume breach mindset, we have to think differently about collaboration. Instead of opening up all interfaces to all teams, we open up the design side to extreme collaboration while restricting operational access at the service layer. This means that any two engineers in the company can get together to share ideas and source code. At the same time, an attacker who gains admin privileges in one service cannot affect another service operating on the same host.

Although it might sound counterintuitive, this actually promotes more collaboration among teams. If you are the on-call DevOps engineer for a service and are diagnosing a failure, you must be able to work seamlessly with other teams to get a complete understanding of the problem. Transactions cross multiple boundaries in the cloud, and failures often emerge from multiple small errors. For this reason, the Microsoft incident response procedures are tuned to encourage cross-team investigative work. Teams that swarm on an issue tend to build more resilient interfaces between those services, improving the overall security and reliability of Azure.

Jim Molini
Senior Program Manager, C+E Security

Azure security architecture

As described earlier in this chapter, cloud security is a shared responsibility, and Azure is no different in this regard. However, Azure was built from a security foundation that uses the Security Development Lifecycle (SDL) principles from the ground up. The Azure platform includes many built-in capabilities that enhance the overall protection of your assets located in Azure.

The Azure infrastructure uses a defense-in-depth approach by implementing security controls in different layers, which expands from physical security, data security, identity and access management, and application security. Figure 1-4 illustrates some of the core architecture components of Azure.

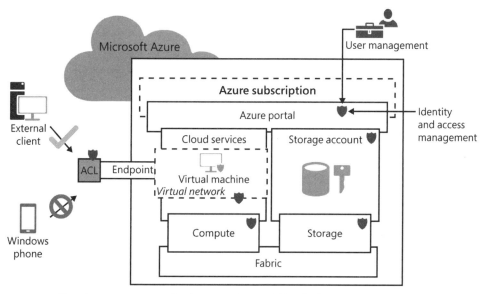

FIGURE 1-4 Core Azure components that have security capabilities built in

The first security control in place is to verify the user's identity by checking the subscription level. The subscription owner or account administrator is the person who signed up for the Azure subscription. This person is authorized to access the account center and perform all management tasks available. In a new subscription, the account administrator is also the service administrator, and this administrator inherits rights to manage the Azure portal. Customers should be very cautious regarding who has access to this account.

> **IMPORTANT** Azure administrators should use Role-Based Access Control (RBAC) provided by Azure to delegate appropriate permission to users. Read more about RBAC at *azure.microsoft.com /documentation/articles/role-based-access-control-configure.*

After the user is authenticated according to her level of authorization, she can manage her resources by using the Azure portal. This is a unified hub that simplifies building, deploying, and managing your cloud resources. The Azure portal also calculates the existing charges and forecasts customers' monthly charges.

A subscription can include zero or more cloud services and zero or more storage accounts. From the Azure portal, you can provision new cloud services, such as a new virtual machine (VM). These VMs use resources allocated from compute and storage components in Azure.

These VMs can work within the Azure infrastructure or they can be publicly available from the Internet. You can secure publish resources available in your VM, such as a web server, and harden the access to this resource by using access control lists (ACLs). You can isolate VMs in the cloud by creating different virtual networks and control traffic between virtual networks by using Network Security Groups (NSGs).

> **MORE INFO**   For more information about Azure Active Directory, see Chapter 2, "Identity protection in Azure." For more information about Network Security Groups, see Chapter 3, "Azure network security."

Going deeper into the Azure layers, you have the Azure fabric. Microsoft is responsible for managing this fabric and securing its resources. This fabric manages compute and storage, allocating resources and ensuring that it can recover in case of a hardware failure. In this level, redundancy and fault tolerance are primordial to deliver the service according to the service level agreement (SLA).

Azure design principles

Azure was fundamentally designed to provide confidentiality, integrity, and availability for the customer's assets located in Azure. These principles are included in different areas of Azure, including operations security. When working with your cloud service provider, you must understand how these principles are used to secure your data.

These principles are important for customers migrating to the cloud. Table 1-1 provides a summary of the rationale behind each principle and the security controls provided by Azure to enforce them.

TABLE 1-1 Design principles, rationales, and security controls

Design principle	Rationale	Security control
Confidentiality	Ensures that the customer's data is accessible only by authorized users or objects	Identity management Isolation Encryption
Integrity	Protects the customer's data (compute and storage) against unauthorized changes	Identity management Isolation Encryption Key management
Availability	Provides numerous levels of redundancy to maximize availability of the customer's data	Storage replication Geo-redundant storage Disaster recovery process Availability sets Load balancer

## CHAPTER 2

Identity protection in Azure

According to the Verizon 2015[1] data breach investigation report, 95 percent of the incidents involved some sort of credential theft from customers' devices. This number shows that it is imperative that any organization that wants to increase its level of security must have a good identity protection strategy in place. The same report shows that in August 2015, 1.2 billion credentials were compromised, which was linked to one of the biggest data breaches in 2015.

Credentials exist on-premises and in the cloud, but they are taken from anywhere by using any device. In this chapter, you learn how to use Microsoft Azure Active Directory (Azure AD) to consolidate your identity management, and how to use Azure AD security capabilities to enhance your overall security strategy for identity protection.

Authentication and authorization

The authentication and authorization process in Azure AD is similar to the process used in your Active Directory Domain Services (AD DS) on-premises. Whereas the authentication goal is to establish and validate a user's digital identity, the authorization goal is to control when and how access is granted to authenticated users.

Because you can use different scenarios to take advantage of AD DS for authentication and authorization, the same applies for Azure AD. Some of the key scenarios are:

- Web browser to web application
- Single-page application (SPA)
- Native application to web API
- Web app to web API
- Daemon or server app to web API

To illustrate the most basic authentication method in Azure AD, you can use a web app (the first scenario in the preceding list) as an example and describe the four major steps that are involved in this authentication:

1. A user is using his device to access an app that uses Azure AD as an authentication and authorization repository.

---

[1] Go to *www.verizonenterprise.com/DBIR/2015* to download this report.

2. The user enters his credentials to sign in to the page. This page uses the Azure AD Authentication Library (ADAL).

3. Assuming that the authentication was successful, Azure AD creates an authentication token and returns a sign-in response to the application. This response is based on the *Reply URL* that was previously configured in the Azure portal.

4. At this point, that app validates the token. To do that, the app uses a public signing key and issuer information available at the federation metadata document for Azure AD. After the application validates the token, Azure AD starts a new session with the user. Although the app developer can control the user's session expiration, by default, the user's session expires when the lifetime of the token issued by Azure AD expires.

> **MORE INFO** For more information about the libraries included in ADAL, go to *https://azure.microsoft.com/en-us/documentation/articles/active-directory-authentication-libraries*.

Azure AD supports several of the most widely used authentication and authorization protocols, including:

- Token and claim types
- Federation metadata
- OAuth 2.0
- OpenID Connect 1.0
- Security Assertion Markup Language (SAML)
- WS-Federation 1.2

Although a strong authentication method is necessary to strengthen your identity protection, ensuring that users are able to access only what they need is a mandatory step. Using an app that supports OAuth 2.0 as an example, the authorization process takes place when Azure AD releases an authorization code to the app. This app presents this authorization code to an authorization server, and the authorization server returns an access token that gives the application permission to access the resource.

> **MORE INFO** For more Azure AD authorization information and code samples, go to *https://msdn.microsoft.com/library/azure/dn645542.aspx*.

Azure hierarchy

To better understand how to manage resources and how to use Role-Based Access Control (RBAC) in Azure, it is important to understand the hierarchy and inheritance in Azure. The basic principle is: access that you grant at parent scope is inherited at child scope. Figure 2-1 provides an illustration of how this hierarchy works in Azure.

In Figure 2-1, you can see that one Azure subscription can be linked with only one Azure AD directory. This hierarchy also shows that each resource group belongs to only one Azure subscription, and although one resource group can have multiple resources, one resource can be bound to only one resource group. These concepts are very important to understand, because, by default, Azure has three basic roles that you can apply to all resource types, and to properly authorize access to resources, you must understand this model.

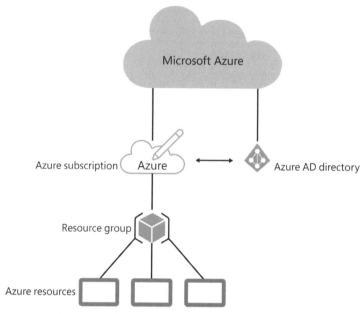

FIGURE 2-1 Azure hierarchy

Role-Based Access Control

Role-Based Access Control (RBAC) is one of the best practices emphasized in the *Security Guidance for Critical Areas of Focus in Cloud Computing V3.0* by Cloud Security Alliance[2]. Most cloud service providers use some sort of RBAC model to administer their resources. Azure helps customers manage their own resources by using RBAC. Some of the key roles available are:

- **Owner** The user added to this role has full access to all resources, which includes the right to delegate access to others.

- **Contributor** The user added to this role is able to create and manage all types of Azure resources; however, the user isn't able to grant access to others.

- **Reader** The user added to this role is able only to view existing Azure resources.

---

[2] You can download this document from *https://downloads.cloudsecurityalliance.org/initiatives/guidance /csaguide.v3.0.pdf.*

MORE INFO For a complete list of built-in Azure roles, go to *https://azure.microsoft.com /documentation/articles/role-based-access-built-in-roles*. To learn more about how to create custom roles, go to *https://azure.microsoft.com/documentation/articles /role-based-access-control-custom-roles*.

Complete the following steps to add a user to a specific role in a resource group by using the Azure portal:

1. Open the Azure portal and sign in with a user account that has owner privileges.

2. In the left navigation bar, select Resource Groups.

3. On the Resource Groups blade, select the resource group that you want to manage, as shown in Figure 2-2.

FIGURE 2-2 Available Azure resource groups

4. When a new blade with the resource group's name opens, select the Access button in the right corner, as shown in Figure 2-3.

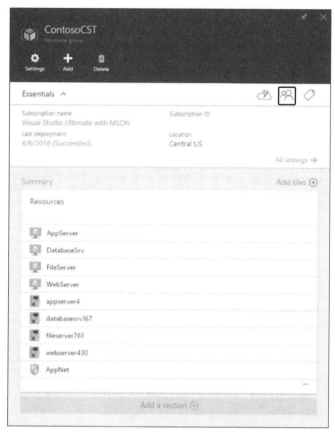

FIGURE 2-3 Resource group options

The Users blade opens, as shown in Figure 2-4.

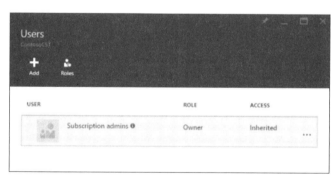

FIGURE 2-4 User role management options

5. At this point, you can manage the available roles by selecting Roles, or you can assign a role to a user. For the purpose of this example, select Add to assign a role to an existing user. On the Add Access blade, select Select A Role, and then select Reader, as shown in Figure 2-5.

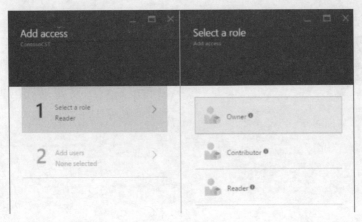

FIGURE 2-5 Selecting a role for an existing user

6. When you select the role, the Select A Role blade automatically closes and you are redirected to the next step on the Add Access blade. Enter the user's name in the search field. When you find the name, select it and then select Select at the bottom of the Add Users blade. Select OK at the bottom of the Add Access blade to close this blade.

The user that you added to this role now appears on the Users blade and the access type is Assigned, as shown in Figure 2-6.

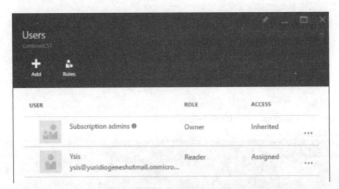

FIGURE 2-6 The Users blade showing the user that was added to the existing role

Although the Azure portal provides this comprehensive approach to manage users and groups, for automation purposes, it is recommended that you use PowerShell to assign roles to users. The following example shows the New-AzureRmRoleAssignment syntax that can be used to assign a role to a user.

```
New-AzureRmRoleAssignment -SignInName <email of user> -RoleDefinitionName <role name in
   quotes> -ResourceGroupName <resource group name>
```

> **MORE INFO** For more information about how to use PowerShell to assign roles to users, go to *https://azure.microsoft.com/en-us/documentation/articles /role-based-access-control-manage-access-powershell*.

On-premises integration

One critical step to enhance the overall identity protection is to ensure that users don't need to be exposed to multiple directories and multiple passwords when they need to access the same resource. Consolidating the authentication experience to allow users to use their credentials to access different cloud apps at the same time as they access on-premises resources is the ideal scenario for identity management.

Azure AD can be integrated with your AD DS located on-premises. Basically, you have two major options for integration. How you perform this integration depends directly on your business needs. The available options are:

- **Directory synchronization with Azure AD Connect**   This enables single identity with the same sign-on experience and password hash synchronization.

- **Azure AD and on-premises Active Directory using federation with Active Directory Federation Services (AD FS)**   This enables single federated identity with single sign-on (SSO).

> **MORE INFO**   For more information about design choices that are directly related to your business requirements, go to *aka.ms/azhidcg* to read the Azure Hybrid Identity Design Considerations Guide.

Azure AD Connect

Azure AD Connect is the preferred option for most scenarios. When you use Azure AD Connect, the users are either created or joined with existing Azure AD accounts. The user's password hash is synchronized from the on-premises AD DS to Azure AD in the cloud. This process is called *password hash sync*.

Azure AD Connect has two scheduler processes that are responsible for synchronizing passwords and general objects and attributes. By default, the scheduler runs every 30 minutes. You can obtain more information about your own schedule by using the PowerShell command Get-ADSyncScheduler.

> **IMPORTANT**   At the time this chapter was written in May 2016, the AD Connect version was 1.1.180.0. Be sure to look for new capabilities and the latest version at *https://azure.microsoft.com /documentation/articles/active-directory-aadconnect-version-history*.

Another built-in security capability in Azure AD Connect is the capability of preventing accidental deletion during synchronization. This capability is enabled by default. The main intent is to avoid synchronizing export operations that have more than 500 deleted records. For example, if an administrator accidentally deletes an entire organizational unit (OU) that has more than 500 accounts, Azure AD Connect will not synchronize these deletions. The administrator receives an email informing her that a completed operation exceeded the configured deletion threshold value. If your organization has a stricter security policy and wants to reduce this value, you can use the PowerShell command Enable-ADSyncExportDeletionThreshold.

Azure AD Connect implementation

Complete the following steps to configure Azure AD Connect to synchronize with your on-premises AD DS:

1. Using an account that has administrative privileges, log on to the computer on which you want to install Azure AD Connect.

2. Download the latest version of Azure AD Connect from *go.microsoft.com /fwlink/?LinkId=615771*.

3. After the download finishes, double-click the file AzureADConnect.msi. The installation process completes quickly.

4. If User Account Control asks for authorization to run the .msi file, select Yes. After the installation finishes, the Welcome To Azure AD Connect page appears. Read the license terms, select I Agree To The License Terms And Privacy Notice, as shown in Figure 2-7, and then select Continue.

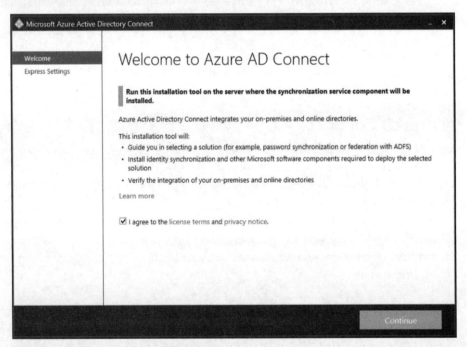

FIGURE 2-7 Azure AD Connect welcome screen

5. On the Express Settings page, select Use Express Settings.

6. On the Connect To Azure AD page (see Figure 2-8), enter your Azure AD credentials. In this case, the user must be a global admin for this process to work. If you use credentials that are not for a member of this group, the installation will fail with an Access Denied error.

7. After you enter the correct credentials, select Next.

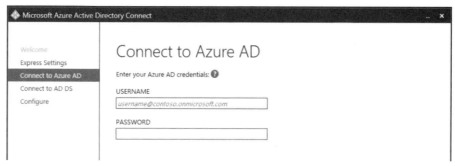

FIGURE 2-8 Credentials to connect to Azure AD

8. On the Connect To AD DS page (see Figure 2-9), enter the on-premises domain creden-tial (DOMAIN\User name). The user needs to have enterprise admin privileges.

FIGURE 2-9 On-premises AD DS credentials

9. After you finish entering the credentials, select Next.
10. On the Ready To Configure page, select Install.

> **IMPORTANT** If you want to perform additional configuration, such as filtering, be sure to clear the Start The Synchronization Process As Soon As Configuration Completes check box. If you clear this check box, the wizard configures sync but leaves the scheduler disabled. In this case, it will not run unless you run the installation wizard again.

11. When the installation finishes, select Exit.

After the synchronization completes, you can validate the synchronization by opening Azure AD, selecting the directory that was synchronized, selecting the Users tab, and verifying that the accounts from your on-premises AD DS synchronized. Notice that the Source From column differentiates between Azure AD and Local Active Directory, as shown in Figure 2-10.

After you install Azure AD Connect, the sync process takes places under a service account created by the installation wizard. This account holds the encryption keys to the database that is used by synchronization. The password for this service account is set to never expire; this behavior should not be changed.

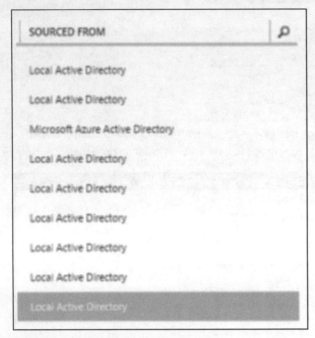

FIGURE 2-10 Source location of the user account

Federation

Although Azure AD Connect is the preferred option to synchronize your on-premises directory with Azure AD, when you have an environment that has multiple domains, federation becomes the most appropriate choice. Other design decisions that might lead you to choose Active Directory Federation Services (AD FS) are as follows:

- Your organization already has an AD FS infrastructure in place and wants to keep control on-premises.
- The organization's security policy prohibits password hash synchronization.
- Your organization requires SSO from domain-joined machines.
- Your organization requires conditional access for on-premises and cloud resources.
- You need to preserve the use of soft account lockout and work hours policies that were configured in your on-premises AD DS.

To implement federation, you need an on-premises federation such as AD FS or another supported solution[3]. Assuming you have the required infrastructure in place, you will also use Azure AD Connect to perform the configuration.

> **IMPORTANT**   If your AD FS and Web Application Proxy servers are behind a firewall, read the article at *https://azure.microsoft.com/documentation/articles/active-directory-aadconnect-ports* to understand which ports should be open.

AD FS implementation

Complete the following steps to configure AD FS synchronization via the Azure AD Connect tool to synchronize with your on-premises AD DS:

1. Using an account that has administrative privileges, log on to the computer on which you want to install Azure AD Connect.

2. Download the latest version of Azure AD Connect from *go.microsoft.com /fwlink/?LinkId=615771*.

3. After the download finishes, double-click the file AzureADConnect.msi. The installation process completes quickly.

4. If User Account Control asks for authorization to run the .msi file, select Yes. After the installation finishes, the Welcome To Azure AD Connect page appears. Read the license terms, select I Agree To The License Terms And Privacy Notice, and then select Continue.

5. On the Express Settings page, select Customize.

6. On the Install Required Components page, leave the default selection, and select Install.

7. On the User Sign-in page, select Federation With AD FS (see Figure 2-11), and then select Next.

    > **IMPORTANT**   Notice that in the lower part of this page, the Azure AD Connect Installation Wizard tells you exactly what is required in order to deploy this configuration. Make sure you comply with these requirements before you move on.

8. On the Connect To Azure AD page, enter your Azure AD credentials. The same account requirements that were specified earlier are applicable here. After entering your credentials, select Next.

---

[3] To find a list of supported solutions, go to *https://azure.microsoft.com/documentation/articles /active-directory-aadconnect-federation-compatibility*.

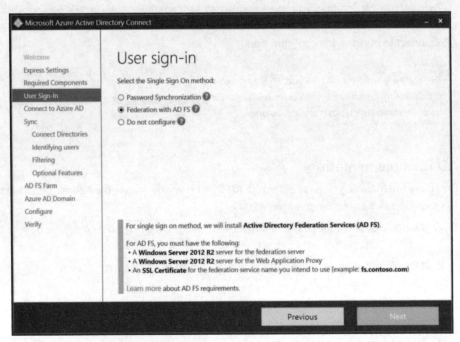

FIGURE 2-11 Selecting federation with AD FS

9. On the Connect Your Directories page (see Figure 2-12), select your forest from the list, enter your AD DS domain credentials, and select Add Directory. If there is no additional directory to add, select Next to proceed.

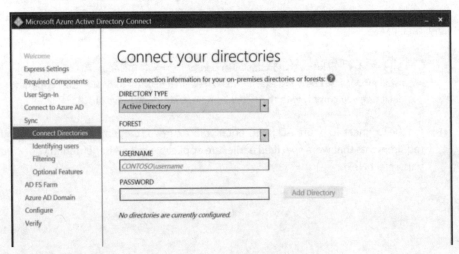

FIGURE 2-12 Selecting the on-premises directory that you want to federate

10. On the Uniquely Identifying Your Users page (see Figure 2-13), you can define how users from your AD DS forests are represented in Azure AD. For this step, use the default option. If you need to customize, the available options are:

- **Users are represented only once across all directories**   Use this option if you want all users to be created as individual objects in Azure AD (default selection).

- **Mail attribute**   Use this option when your contacts have been created by using GALSync.

- **ObjectSID and msExchangeMasterAccountSID/ msRTCSIP-OriginatorSid**   Use this option if you want to join an enabled user account in an account forest with a disabled user account in a Microsoft Exchange resource forest.

- **SAMAccountName and MailNickName**   Use this option if you want to join attributes where the sign-in ID for the user can be found.

- **A specific attribute**   Use this option if you want to customize your own attribute.

- **Source anchor**   The source anchor attribute is an immutable (cannot change) attribute that will always be the same during the object's lifetime[4]. If you choose this option, be sure to use a unique attribute.

- **User principal name**   This attribute is used by users when they sign in to Azure AD and Microsoft Office 365.

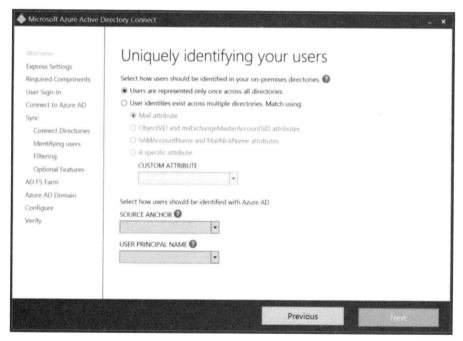

FIGURE 2-13 Customizing how your users will be identified

---

[4] For more information regarding the immutable attribute, see *https://azure.microsoft.com/documentation/articles /active-directory-aadconnect-design-concepts*.

11. On the Filter Users And Devices page, leave Synchronize All Users And Devices selected and select Next.

12. On the Optional Features page, leave the default selection and select Next.

13. On the AD FS Farm page (see Figure 2-14), select Configure A New Windows Server 2012 R2 AD FS Farm if you don't have an AD FS infrastructure on-premises or if your current infrastructure doesn't meet the requirements. If your current infrastructure meets the requirements, select Use An Existing Windows Server 2012 R2 AD FS Farm. For this step, leave the first option selected and select Browse to select the certificate (PFX file).

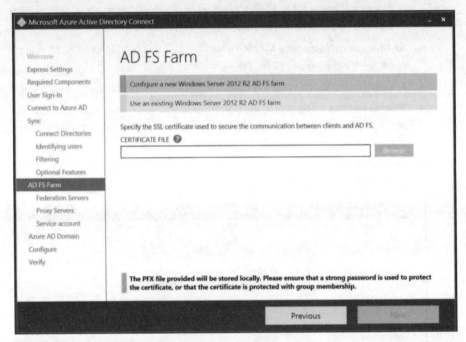

FIGURE 2-14 Selecting the AD FS server

14. When the Certificate Password dialog box opens, enter the certificate's password, select OK, and then select Next.

> **IMPORTANT** If the certificate you selected has multiple subject names or it is a wildcard certificate, you can select the correct subject name from the Subject Name list; in this case, you also need to specify the subject name prefix.

15. On the AD FS Server page, enter the fully qualified domain name of the server that you want to use as a federation server, select Add, and then select Next to proceed. At this point, the Azure AD Connect Wizard validates the server, and if the user that you specified earlier is not a local admin in this server, the wizard prompts you for credentials.

16. On the Web Application Proxy Servers page, enter the fully qualified domain name of your Web Application Proxy Server, select Add, and then select Next.

17. On the Proxy Trust Credentials page, enter the credentials that the Web Application Proxy Server will use to connect to the AD FS Server. This user needs to be a local administrator on the AD FS server. After entering the credentials, select Next.

18. On the AD FS Service Account page (see Figure 2-15), specify the AD FS domain service account that you will use to authenticate users and to look up user information in Active Directory. You can select Create A Group Managed Service Account if you already have Windows Server 2012 domain controllers in the domain that AD FS servers will belong to. If you do not have Windows Server 2012 domain controllers in the domain, select Use A Domain User Account.

FIGURE 2-15 Selecting the appropriated AD FS service account according to your environment

19. After you make the selection based on your environment, select Next.

20. On the Azure AD Domain page, in the list, select the domain that you want to federate. This option sets up the federation relationship between AD FS and Azure AD. It configures AD FS to issue security tokens to Azure AD and configures Azure AD to trust the tokens from this specific AD FS instance. After you finish selecting the domain, select Next.

21. On the Ready To Configure page, leave Start The Synchronization Process As Soon As The Configuration Completes selected if you want to perform this sync right away. You can also select Enable Staging Mode if you want to set up a new sync server in parallel with an existing server. For this step, leave the default selection and select Install.

22. On the Installation Complete page, review the results, and then select Verify to force Azure AD Connect to verify the DNS settings for you. After you finish the verification, select Exit.

Suspicious activity identification

In the cloud-first, mobile-first world, it is expected that you will have users signing in from different devices and from different locations. Another important identity management principle is that you should be able to monitor users' signing behavior to identify suspicious activities. Azure AD Premium[5] access and usage reports are based on machine learning and help you to easily monitor and protect access to your Azure Active Directory tenant resources.

> **IMPORTANT** For more information about the different Azure AD editions, go to *https://azure.microsoft.com/documentation/articles/active-directory-editions*.

IT administrators can use these reports to view information that will help them make the organization's resources more secure. The data collected and displayed by Azure AD Premium reports can be used to better determine where possible security risks might be present so that they can be addressed and mitigated. As shown in Figure 2-16, Azure AD Premium reports monitor user access habits and usual behaviors; some reports use the power and the worldwide presence of Azure AD with billions of authentications every day and information from the Microsoft Digital Crimes Unit.

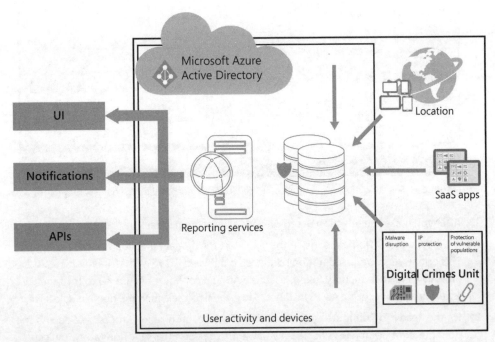

FIGURE 2-16 Azure AD Premium reports mechanism

---

[5] To get started with Azure AD Premium, go to *https://azure.microsoft.com/documentation/articles /active-directory-get-started-premium*.

By cross-checking and synthesizing this information, Azure tries to identify infected devices or IPs that try to infect others. This information is compared with the access attempts to every organizations' resources and provides a view of all devices or IPs that were reported infected in the past few weeks and are accessing applications published via Azure AD.

To view the reports available for you to run, open the Azure portal and go to the Reports tab of your Azure AD directory. You should see a screen similar to Figure 2-17.

FIGURE 2-17 Azure AD premium reports

The report has four sections, and each section has details about what type of information you can obtain. The most relevant reports for incident response are available in the Anomalous Activity section.

To run a report, select the report name in the list, which takes you to a detailed page for that specific report. In addition to viewing the report, you can download a copy of it as a compressed, comma-separated values (CSVs) format for offline viewing or backup purposes.

By default, Azure AD retrieves information from the last 30 days for reporting purposes. If no anomaly appears in the report that you selected, you get a result similar to what's shown in Figure 2-18.

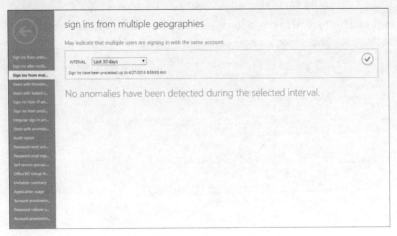

FIGURE 2-18 Sign Ins From Multiple Geographies report result

Identity protection

The beginning of this chapter emphasized how important it is to keep your identity secure, mainly because of the growing number of attacks targeting users' credentials. Azure AD Identity Protection uses the Azure AD anomaly detection capabilities (shown in the previous section) and triggers risk events that can help you to identify suspicious activities. This goes beyond the reporting capabilities, because it helps you to see anomalies affecting an organization's identity in real time.

> **IMPORTANT**   At the time this chapter was written, this feature was in public preview and it was available only for users in the United States region.

The Identity Protection capability in Azure AD works by calculating a user risk level for each user. You can use it to configure risk-based policies to automatically protect the identities of your organization. By using these risk-based policies, in addition to other conditional access controls provided by Azure Active Directory and Enterprise Mobility Suite (EMS), you can automatically block access or provide remediation actions, such as password resets and Azure Multi-Factor Authentication enforcement.

Complete the following steps to access Azure AD Identity Protection. Keep in mind that these steps use Azure AD Identity Protection Public Preview, which requires installation via Marketplace:

1. Open the Azure portal, select Browse in the left navigation pane, enter **Marketplace**, and when it appears, select it.

2. In the search box, on the Everything blade, enter **Azure AD Identity Protection**, and when it appears, select it. When the Azure AD Identity Protection blade appears, select Create.

3. Select the Azure AD directory that you want, to enable Azure AD Identity Protection, and select Create.

4. Open the Azure portal, select Browse in the left navigation pane, and enter **Azure AD Identity Protection**. The Azure AD Identity Protection dashboard appears (see Figure 2-19). Note that when you first add Azure AD Identity Protection, the dashboard might not be populated with information.

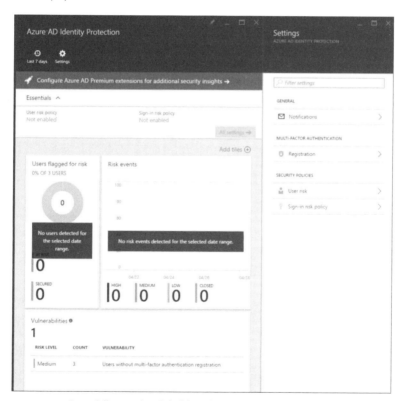

FIGURE 2-19 A partially populated dashboard

The sections that follow explore in more detail the options available in each section of this dashboard.

Identity protection with Azure AD

Credential compromise is the single biggest risk to your infrastructure, allowing unauthorized users to get access they can exploit for lateral attacks and incremental escalation of privilege, eventually resulting in full control of your resources. Azure Active Directory identity-driven security capabilities, by using user behavioral analysis, advanced machine-learning technologies, and the power of the Microsoft Digital Crimes Unit, are helping protect the cloud identities of thousands of enterprises. By gathering and analyzing signals from billions of authentications and malicious attacks against every Microsoft online service all over the world, enterprise and consumer, Azure Active Directory can effectively help protect your business.

Azure Active Directory Identity Protection takes identity protection to the next level by detecting attacks in real time, informing you of risks and applying controls to keep your enterprise safe.

In detection, signal is everything. Microsoft is uniquely positioned as a major consumer, enterprise identity, and email provider to see attacks in varieties and volumes most others simply can't. If unauthorized users get their hands on a set of user name/password pairs—through breach of another site, phishing, or malware—they will likely test those credentials against the major mail-providing identity providers (IdPs) in hopes that the credentials link to other websites, banks, file storage—anything they can exploit for value. Every day, we analyze tens of terabytes of logs resulting from 14 billion logon events.

This signal is combined with signals from services like Microsoft Exchange Server, SharePoint, Skype, and OneDrive to further strengthen our analysis. We also benefit from research from teams like the Digital Crimes Unit and Microsoft Security Response Center, law enforcement, academia, security researchers, and industry partners.

Finally, our attackers help us, because we detect more than 10,000 attacker-controlled IP addresses, and detect and block more than 10 million bogus logon attempts per day, resulting in 1.5 million newly protected credential pairs every day. This results in world-class signal and battle-tested algorithms that you can use to protect your identity infrastructure.

Azure Active Directory Identity Protection uses all this data, analysis, and experience to generate user and logon risk scores, then use these to notify you of compromised users, risky logons, and configuration vulnerabilities in your environment before they can be exploited by cyber criminals. By providing a consolidated view into risks, remediation recommendations, and in-line response options, we empower you to better protect your organization. The service uses advanced machine learning to detect suspicious activities based on signals including brute force attacks, leaked credentials, sign-ins from unfamiliar locations, and infected devices. This investment in real-time threat detection is what helps us meet our goal of preventing attacks from being effective in the first place.

The Azure AD Identity Protection signal can be configured to trigger Risk-Based Conditional Access policies that automatically respond to threats by blocking logons, issuing Azure Active Directory Multi-Factor Authentication challenges, or if the evidence is strong enough, requiring the users to change their credentials. For example, if our machine learning system believes that a logon is coming from a new, anonymized, or bot-controlled network location, Conditional Access auto-remediation can intercept the request with an adaptive two-factor challenge. If our threat intelligence or advanced machine-learning algorithms indicate that a user's credentials are compromised, policies can offer automatic remediation in the form of blocking the account or, with Multi-Factor Authentication, requiring a user-initiated password change.

Azure AD Identity Protection also helps you identify and remediate configuration vulnerabilities, and integrates with Azure AD Privileged Identity Management, Cloud App Discovery, and Multi-Factor Authentication to improve your security posture.

Nasos Kladakis
Sr. Product Marketing Manager. Identity and Access Management

User risk policy

This is the first policy you should enable. The intent of this policy is to remediate user risk by requiring users to perform Multi-Factor Authentication and change their passwords. To enforce that, Azure AD Identity Protection verifies potential risk events, which are events that were flagged as suspicious activity and indicate that an identity might have been compromised. The risks identified by Azure AD Identity Protection are:

- Leaked credentials.
- Impossible travel to atypical locations.
- Sign-ins from infected devices.
- Sign-ins from anonymous IP addresses.
- Sign-ins from IP addresses with suspicious activity.
- Signs in from unfamiliar locations.

Complete the following steps to enable this policy:

1. With the Azure AD Identity Protection dashboard open, under User Risk Policy, verify that Not Enabled is selected (see Figure 2-20).

FIGURE 2-20 Risk Policy that needs to be changed

The User Risk blade appears, as shown in Figure 2-21.

FIGURE 2-21 Options available for user risk policy

2. Under Set Scope, select Included to display the Included blade. Select Add (plus sign), and then add the users that you want to be monitored by this policy. If you want to enable this policy for all users, select On next to All Users.

3. After you finish adding the users, on the Included blade, select Done.

4. The next option is the Risk Level For Password Change. A user risk level is an indication (High, Medium, or Low) of the likelihood that the user's identity has been compromised. Azure AD Identity Protection calculates this based on the user risk events that are associated with the user's identity. If your organization has a very strict security policy, choose Medium, which forces the user to enable Multi-Factor Authentication if the risk is medium or higher. For the purpose of completing this step, select Medium.

5. The next option is Risk Level For Blocking Sign-In. The same rationale applies here regarding how the calculation is performed; the difference is that, in this case, if the user reaches this risk level, he will not be able to sign in. For the purpose of completing this step, select Medium.

6. Select On to enable this security policy.

7. At the top of the blade, select Save.

Now that the risk policy is enabled, it is important to emphasize that risk events are either identified in real time, or in post-processing after the risk event has already taken place (offline). When this chapter was written and this feature was in Public Preview, most risk events were computed offline and showed up in Azure AD Identity Protection within two to four hours. For those evaluated in real time, they will show up in the Azure AD Identity Protection dashboard within 5 to 10 minutes.

Sign-in risk policy

The intent of the sign-in risk policy is to detect the likelihood that for a specific sign-in, someone else is attempting to authenticate with the user's identity. The risk level previously explained is also applicable for this policy, and it is evaluated at the time of a sign-in. This policy is applicable for all browser traffic and sign-ins; however, it is not applicable to applications using older security protocols by disabling the WS-Trust endpoint at the federated identity providers (IdPs), such as AD FS.

To enable this policy, under Sign-in Risk Policy, select Not Enabled, as shown in Figure 2-22, and follow the same steps that were explained previously for user risk policy.

FIGURE 2-22 Sign-in risk policy that needs to be changed

When you enable this policy, keep in mind that selecting High as your threshold reduces the number of times a policy is triggered and minimizes the impact to users. At the same time, it excludes Low and Medium sign-ins flagged for risk from the policy, which might not block an attacker from exploiting a compromised identity. Keep the balance according to your environment needs and organization-wide security policy requirements.

Notification enabling

Now that both policies are configured, the next step is to ensure that you receive notifications in case an account is compromised. User-compromised alert email is one type of email that is generated by Azure AD Identity Protection; the other type is the weekly digest email, which contains the following:

- Users at risk
- Suspicious activities
- Detected vulnerabilities
- Links to the related reports in Azure AD Identity Protection

To enable email notification, select Settings in the Azure AD Identity Protection dashboard. On the Settings blade, select Notifications. Under Weekly Email Digest, select On, as shown in Figure 2-23, and then select Save.

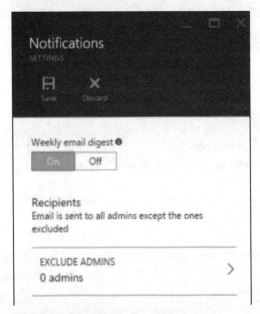

FIGURE 2-23 Enabling email notifications

Vulnerabilities

The vulnerabilities section of Azure AD Identity Protection helps you to quickly identify potential identity risks. Figure 2-24 shows an example of how the Vulnerabilities tile looks after a vulnerability is found.

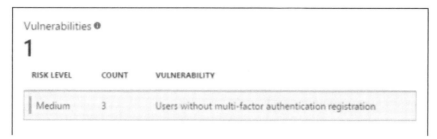

FIGURE 2-24 Vulnerabilities tile showing the number of occurrences and the risk level

This brief report shows the number of vulnerabilities that were found (one in this case), the number of occurrences for this particular vulnerability (three in this case), and the type of vulnerability (missing Multi-Factor Authentication). Selecting the vulnerability displays its remediation, which in this case is to enable Multi-Factor Authentication, as shown in Figure 2-25.

FIGURE 2-25 Remediation for this vulnerability

Multi-Factor Authentication

In the previous section of this book, you read that Azure AD Identity Protection is capable of enforcing Azure Multi-Factor Authentication via security policies. This is an important step toward identity protection. Ideally, all users are already using Multi-Factor Authentication, because nowadays it is not recommended to rely only on a user name and password to verify a user's authenticity.

With Multi-Factor Authentication, you force users to provide something that they know (password or PIN), something that they have (a phone, card, or hardware token), and something that they are (fingerprint, retina scan, or other biometric). Figure 2-26 illustrates the Multi-Factor Authentication flow.

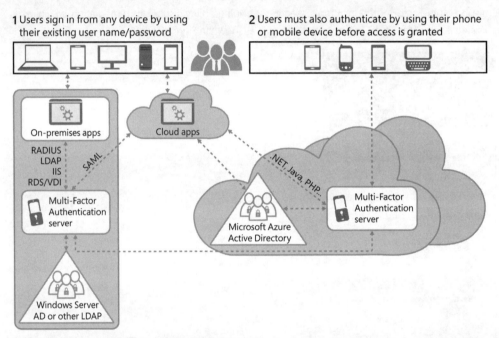

FIGURE 2-26 Azure Multi-Factor Authentication flow

The illustration shows users using different devices to sign in. The directory can be on-premises, in the cloud, or both (hybrid). In a hybrid environment, you can use your on-premises directory to perform the authentication, for example, if you are using AD FS to federate with Azure AD. You also have the option to use a Multi-Factor Authentication server on-premises[6] to keep the Multi-Factor Authentication process on-premises.

There are many Multi-Factor Authentication options, including Multi-Factor Authentication for Office 365, Multi-Factor Authentication for Azure Administrators, and Azure Multi-Factor Authentication.

---

[6] To learn how to install and configure an on-premises Multi-Factor Authentication server, go to *https://azure.microsoft.com/documentation/videos/multi-factor-authentication-server*.

This section of the book covers Azure Multi-Factor Authentication, which has the richest set of capabilities and provides additional configuration options via the Azure Management portal, such as advanced reporting and support for a range of on-premises and cloud apps. This version of Azure Multi-Factor Authentication comes as part of Azure Active Directory Premium.

> **MORE INFO**   For design considerations regarding Azure Multi-Factor Authentication, go to *https://azure.microsoft.com/documentation/articles /active-directory-hybrid-identity-design-considerations-multifactor-auth-requirements*.

Azure Multi-Factor Authentication provides additional security by requiring a second form of authentication, and it supports a range of verification options, which are as follows:

- **Phone call**   This method triggers a call to the user's phone and asks for a verification number. This verification number is assigned by the user during the Multi-Factor Authentication registration process.

- **Text message**   Using this method, the user receives a text message that has a six-digit number that needs to be entered during the authentication process.

- **Mobile app notification**   In this method, a verification request is sent to a user's phone, asking her to complete the verification by selecting Verify From The Mobile App.

- **Mobile app verification code**   For this method, a verification code is sent to the mobile app that is running on a user's smartphone.

Before you implement Azure Multi-Factor Authentication, you must understand what options are available to obtain this capability. If your license is for Azure AD Premium, Enterprise Mobility Suite, or Enterprise Cloud Suite, you automatically get Azure Multi-Factor Authentication. If you don't have it, you can purchase separate Azure Multi-Factor Authentication licenses and assign them to your users.

You can have *per user* usage, which is a good option for organizations that want to license a fixed number of users, or you can have *per authentication* usage. This method is ideal for a scenario in which an organization has users who infrequently need authentication.

Azure Multi-Factor Authentication implementation

The Azure Multi-Factor Authentication implementation covered in this section is the cloud-based implementation. This implementation is basically three primary steps (assuming that you already have an Azure subscription). These steps are:

1. Create the Azure Multi-Factor Authentication provider.

2. Enable Azure Multi-Factor Authentication for your users.

3. Notify the users about Multi-Factor Authentication.

Complete the following steps to enable Azure Multi-Factor Authentication in the cloud for users:

1. Open the Azure portal, select Browse, and then select Active Directory.

2. When you are redirected to the classic portal, select Active Directory in the left navigation pane, and then select Multi-Factor Auth Providers. If you are doing this process for the first time, you should see something similar to what's shown in Figure 2-27.

FIGURE 2-27 Creating a new Multi-Factor Authentication provider

3. Select Create A New Multi-Factor Authentication Provider. The options to create a new provider appear at the bottom of the window, as shown in Figure 2-28.

FIGURE 2-28 Selecting the options to create a new provider

4. In the Name box, enter the name for this provider. In the Usage Model list, select Per Authentication or Per Enabled User. Notice the warning that says that after you select this method, you cannot change it.

5. In the Directory box, select the directory you want to link this provider to.

6. Select Create to display a screen similar to what's shown in Figure 2-29.

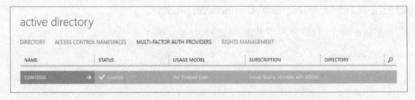

FIGURE 2-29 Multi-Factor Authentication provider successfully created

7. Go to the Directory tab, select the directory in which you enabled the Multi-Factor Authentication provider, the directory where you want to enable Azure Multi-Factor Authentication, and then go to the Users tab.

8. In the lower part of the window, select Manage Multi-Factor Auth Status to display the Multi-Factor Authentication page (see Figure 2-30).

FIGURE 2-30 Selecting users to enable Azure Multi-Factor Authentication

9. The bottom part of this window might vary because it will show the users that are in your directory. Beside each user is a check box that you can select to enable Azure Multi-Factor Authentication for that particular user. You can select the Display Name check box if you want to enable it for all users. After you select the user, under Quick Steps, select Enable.

10. When a dialog box opens, asking you to confirm that you want to enable Azure Multi-Factor Authentication for that user, select Enable Multi-Factor Auth. In the Updates Successful dialog box, select Close.

After you finish enabling Azure Multi-Factor Authentication for the users, you should notify them about this change. This notification usually is done via email, and the following instructions should be included:

1. Sign in to the Office 365 Portal at *portal.microsoftonline.com*.

2. Follow the instructions to set up your preferred Multi-Factor Authentication method when signing in to Office 365 by using a web browser.

3. Create one app password for each device.

4. Enter the same app password in all applicable apps (such as Microsoft Outlook, Mail client, Lync, Word, PowerPoint, Excel, and Dynamics CRM) on that device.

5. Update your Office client applications or other mobile applications to use an app password.

The email should also explain why the organization is enforcing this policy and should include your support service contact information.

Azure Multi-Factor Authentication option configuration

After configuring Azure Multi-Factor Authentication, you can customize some options. To access these options, go back to the Manage Azure MFA option and select Service Settings. Figure 2-31 shows the available options.

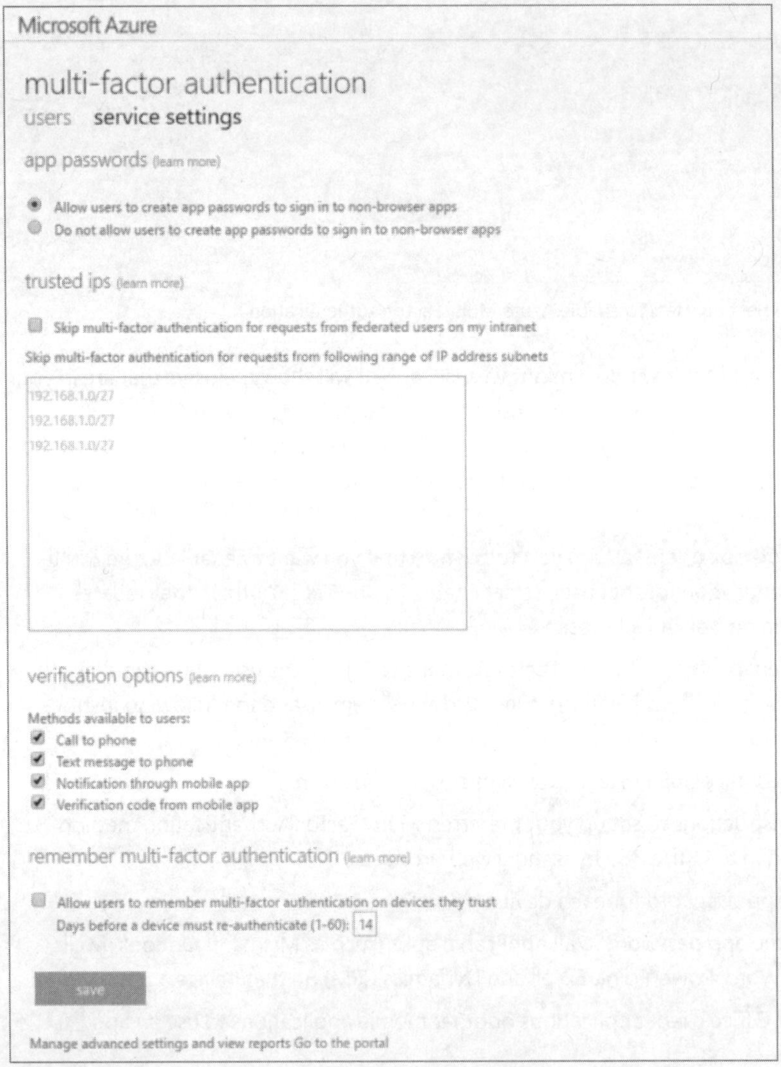

FIGURE 2-31 Azure Multi-Factor Authentication options

This window has four sections; each section has its own set of customizable options. The default selection in App Passwords is configured to allow users to create app passwords to sign in. Although this option provides greater flexibility, you should keep in mind that when users can have multiple app passwords, the likelihood of theft increases: the more apps that deal with passwords, the greater the attack surface.

Also be careful with apps[7] that cache passwords. When used in on-premises scenarios, authentication might fail because the app password is known outside of the organizational ID.

In the second section of this window, you can configure a list of trusted IPs. This is particularly useful if you have some locations where you trust the source IP and do not want to enforce Multi-Factor Authentication for traffic coming from that location. In the third section, you can configure the verification options, which are the available validation options for the users. By default, all options are selected, but you can customize it and leave enabled only those that you want to implement in your environment.

The last option provides the capability of remembering Multi-Factor Authentication from trusted devices. In this case, you can enforce the number of days that this information is cached before it expires. After you finish configuring these options, select Save.

---

[7] For more options regarding app passwords, go to *https://azure.microsoft.com/documentation/articles /multi-factor-authentication-whats-next/#app-passwords*.

## CHAPTER 3

Azure network security

To understand Microsoft Azure network security, you have to know all the pieces and parts that are included. That means this chapter begins with a description and definition of all the features and services related to Azure networking that are relevant to security. For each feature, the chapter describes what it is and provides some examples to help you understand what the feature does and why it's good (or bad) at what it does. Some capabilities in Azure networking don't have a security story to tell, so the chapter leaves out those capabilities.

After the groundwork is laid and you have a better understanding of Azure networking, the chapter discusses Azure security best practices. These best practices are a compilation of things that you should do regarding Azure network security if they are appropriate to your deployment.

The chapter ends with a description of some useful patterns that you might want to use as reference implementation examples on which you can build your own solutions.

The goal of this chapter is to help you understand the "what's" and "why's," because if you don't understand those, you'll never get to the how's; if you implement the "how's" without understanding the "what's" and the "why's," you'll end up with the same "it sort of grew that way" network that you might have on-premises today. (If your network isn't like that, consider yourself exceptionally wise or lucky.)

To summarize, the chapter:

- Discusses the components of Azure networking from a security perspective.
- Goes over a collection of Azure networking best practices.
- Describes some Azure network security patterns that you might want to adopt for your own deployments.

One more thing before you venture into the inner workings of Azure networking: If you've been with Azure for a while, you're probably aware that Azure started with the Azure Service Management (ASM) model for managing resources. Even if you haven't been around Azure since the beginning, you're probably aware of the "old" and "new" portals (the "old" portal is now called the "classic" portal and the new portal is called the "Azure portal"). The classic portal uses the ASM model. The new portal uses the resource management model known as Azure Resource Management. This chapter focuses only on the Azure Resource Management model and the networking capabilities and behavior related to this model.

The reason for this is that the ASM model is being phased out and there is no future in it, so it would be best to migrate your ASM assets (if you have any) to the new Azure Resource Management model.

> **MORE INFO**   For more information about the differences between the ASM and Azure Resource Management models, read the article "Azure Resource Manager vs. classic deployment: Understand deployment models and the state of your resources" at *https://azure.microsoft.com /documentation/articles/resource-manager-deployment-model*.

Anatomy of Azure networking

Azure networking has a lot of moving parts, and figuring out what these different parts do can be intimidating. The networking documentation on *Azure.com* focuses on the names of the products, and unfortunately these product names do not always make it easy for you to intuit the functionality of the product or feature. (Of course, this isn't just an Azure networking problem; you can go to any major cloud service provider's site and be assailed with the same problem.)

For this reason, this section is broken down into headings that focus on the capability you're interested in. For example, instead of providing the product name "Azure ExpressRoute" (which is explained later in detail), the heading for that networking capability is "Cross-premises connectivity." Because most people in networking know what that is, you don't need to try to figure it out from a product name. This format should help you understand what Azure has to offer in the networking arena.

This section describes the following Azure networking capabilities:

- Virtual network infrastructure
- Network access control
- Routing tables
- Remote access
- Cross-premises connectivity
- Network availability
- Network logging
- Public name resolution
- Network security appliances
- Reverse proxy

Virtual network infrastructure

Before getting into the Microsoft Azure Virtual Network itself, you should know that all servers that you deploy in Azure are actually virtual machines (VMs). This is important to understand, because some people new to the cloud might think that a public cloud service provider like Microsoft offers dedicated hardware servers as a service.

With the understanding that you use VMs to host servers in Azure, the question is, how do those VMs connect to a network? The answer is that VMs connect to an Azure Virtual Network.

Azure Virtual Networks are similar to virtual networks that have virtualization platform solutions, such as Microsoft Hyper-V or VMware. Hyper-V is used in Azure, so you can take advantage of the Hyper-V virtual switch for networking. You can think of the Hyper-V virtual switch as representing a virtual network interface that a VM's virtual network interface connects to.

One thing that might be different than what you use on-premises is how Microsoft isolates one customer's network from another customer's network. On-premises, you might use different virtual switches to separate different networks from each other, and that's perfectly reasonable. You can do that because you control the entire network stack and the IP addressing scheme on your network, in addition to the entire routing infrastructure. In Azure, Microsoft can't give each customer that level of control because Microsoft needs to reuse the same private IP address space among all the different customers, and Microsoft can't tell each customer which segment of the private IP address space to use for their VMs.

To get around this challenge, Microsoft takes advantage of the Windows Server software-defined networking stack—also known as "Hyper-V Network Virtualization" (HNV). With HNV, Microsoft can isolate each customer's network from other customer networks by encapsulating each customer's network communications within a generic routing encapsulation (GRE) head that contains a field that is specifically for the customer. This effectively isolates each customer's network from the others, even if different customers are using the same IP address schemes on their Azure Virtual Networks.

> **MORE INFO** For more information about Hyper-V network virtualization, read the article "Hyper-V Network Virtualization Overview" on TechNet at *https://technet.microsoft.com/library /jj134230(v=ws.11).aspx.*

Azure Virtual Network provides you with the following basic capabilities:

- IP address scheme
- Dynamic Host Configuration Protocol (DHCP) server
- Domain Name System (DNS) server

IP address scheme

Azure Virtual Networks require you to use private IP addresses (RFC 1918) for VMs. The address ranges are:

- Class A: 10.0.0.0/24
- Class B: 172.16.0.0/12
- Class C: 192.168.1.0/24

You should create an Azure Virtual Network before you create a VM, because all VMs need to be placed on an Azure Virtual Network. Just like with on-premises networking, you should carefully consider which IP address scheme you want to use, especially if you think you will connect your Azure Virtual Network to your on-premises network. In that scenario, you should make sure there is no overlap between the IP addresses you use on-premises and those you want to use on an Azure Virtual Network.

When you create an Azure Virtual Network, you'll typically choose a large block (or the entire Class A, B, or C range in the preceding list). Then you'll subnet that range, just as you do on-premises.

From a security perspective, you should think about how many subnets you need and how large to make them, because you'll want to create access controls between them. Some organizations use subnets to define security zones, and then create network access controls between the subnets by using Network Security Groups (which is explained later) or a virtual appliance.

Another type of addressing you should consider is public addresses. When you create a VM, a public address is assigned to that VM. Note that the public address isn't bound to the actual network interface (although it might appear that way when you see the description in the portal or read the documentation). The public IP address is the address that external users or devices can use to connect to the VM from over the Internet.

Similar to the IP addresses that are actually bound to the network interfaces on the VM itself (explained in the next section), you can assign either a dynamic or static public IP address to a VM.

Dynamic IP addresses on a public interface aren't as much of a problem as they might be on the internal network—that is to say, on the Azure Virtual Network itself. The reason for this is that DNS is used for Internet name resolution, and few (if any) users or devices are dependent on a static IP address to reach an Internet-reachable resource.

However, there might be situations where you need to use a static IP address on the Internet. For example, you might have network security devices that have access controls so that specific protocols or source IP addresses are allowed access only to specific IP addresses in Azure. When that is the case, you should take advantage of static public IP addresses.

Other scenarios where static public IP addresses might be used include the following:

- You've deployed applications that require communications to an IP address instead of a DNS name.
- You want to avoid having to remap DNS entries for publicly accessible resources on an Azure Virtual Network.

- Applications deployed on Azure or other public or private cloud networks need to use static addresses to communicate with your services on an Azure Virtual Network.
- You use SSL certificates that are dependent on a static IP address.

> **MORE INFO**   To learn more about Azure Virtual Networks, read the article "Virtual Network Overview" at *https://azure.microsoft.com/documentation/articles/virtual-networks-overview*.

DHCP servers

After you create an Azure Virtual Network and then place a VM on the network, the VM needs to have an IP address assigned to it to communicate with other VMs on the Azure Virtual Network (in addition to communicating to on-premises resources and even the Internet).

You can assign two types of IP addresses to VMs:

- Dynamic addresses
- Static addresses

Both types of addresses are managed by an Azure DHCP server.

Dynamic addresses are typically DHCP addresses that are assigned and managed by the Azure DHCP server. Like any other DHCP-assigned address, the VM's address is assigned from the pool of addresses defined by the address space you chose for your Azure Virtual Network.

In most cases, the address won't change over time and you can restart the VM and it will keep the same IP address. However, there might be times when the VM needs to be moved to another host in the Azure fabric, and this might lead to the IP address changing. If you have a server that requires a permanent IP address, then do not use dynamic addressing for that VM.

For VMs that perform roles requiring a static IP address, you can assign a static IP address to the VM. Keep in mind that you do not configure the NIC within the VM to use a static IP address. In fact, you should never touch the NIC configuration settings within a VM. All IP addressing information should be configured within the Azure portal or by using PowerShell Remoting in Azure.

Examples of VMs that might need dedicated addresses include:

- Domain controllers.
- Anything that needs a static address to support firewall rules you might configure on an Azure Virtual Network appliance.
- VMs that are referenced by hard-coded settings requiring IP addresses.
- DNS servers you deploy on an Azure Virtual Network (discussed in the next section).

Keep in mind that you cannot bring your own DHCP server. The VMs are automatically configured to use only the DHCP server provided by Azure.

> **MORE INFO**   For more information on IP addressing in Azure, read the article "IP addresses in Azure" at *https://azure.microsoft.com/documentation/articles /virtual-network-ip-addresses-overview-arm*.

DNS servers

You can use two primary methods for name resolution on an Azure Virtual Network:

- Azure DNS server
- Your own DNS server

When you create an Azure Virtual Network, you get a simple DNS server in the bargain, at no extra charge. This simple DNS server service provides you with basic name resolution for all VMs on the same Azure Virtual Network. Name resolution does not extend outside of the Azure Virtual Network.

The simple Azure Virtual Network DNS is not configurable. You can't create your own A records, SRV records, or any other kind of record. If you need more flexibility than simple name resolution, you should bring your own DNS server.

You can install your own DNS server on an Azure Virtual Network. The DNS server can be a Microsoft standalone DNS server, an Active Directory–integrated DNS server, or a non–Windows-based DNS server. Unlike the situation with DHCP servers on an Azure Virtual Network, you are encouraged to deploy your own DNS servers if you need them.

The bring-your-own-device (BYOD) DNS server is commonly used when you want to create a hybrid network, where you connect your on-premises network with your Azure Virtual Network. In this way, VMs are able to resolve names of devices on your on-premises network, and devices on your on-premises network are able to resolve names of resources you've placed on an Azure Virtual Network.

Network access control

Network access control is as important on Azure Virtual Networks as it is on-premises. The principle of least privilege applies on-premises and in the cloud. One way you do enforce network access controls in Azure is by taking advantage of Network Security Groups (NSGs).

The name might be a little confusing. When you hear "Network Security Group," you might think it's related to a collection of network devices that are grouped in a way that allows for common or centralized security management. Or maybe you'd think such a group might be a collection of VMs that belong to the same security zone. Both of these assumptions would be wrong.

A Network Security Group is the equivalent of a simple stateful packet filtering firewall or router. This is similar to the type of firewalling that was done in the 1990s. That is not said to be negative about NSGs, but to make it clear that some techniques of network access control have survived the test of time.

The "Group" part of the NSG name refers to a group of firewall rules that you configure for the NSG. This group of rules defines allow and deny decisions that the NSG uses to allow or deny traffic for a particular source or destination.

NSGs use a 5-tuple to evaluate traffic:

- Source and destination IP address
- Source and destination port
- Protocol: transmission control protocol (TCP) or user datagram protocol (UDP)

This means you can control access between a single VM and a group of VMs, or a single VM to another single VM, or between entire subnets. Again, keep in mind that this is simple stateful packet filtering, not full packet inspection. There is no protocol validation or network level intrusion detection system (IDS) or intrusion prevention system (IPS) capability in a Network Security Group.

An NSG comes with some built-in rules that you should be aware of. These are:

- **Allow all traffic within a specific virtual network**   All VMs on the same Azure Virtual Network can communicate with each other.
- **Allow Azure load balancing inbound**   This rule allows traffic from any source address to any destination address for the Azure load balancer.
- **Deny all inbound**   This rule blocks all traffic sourcing from the Internet that you haven't explicitly allowed.
- **Allow all traffic outbound to the Internet**   This rule allows VMs to initiate connections to the Internet. If you do not want these connections initiated, you need to create a rule to block those connections or enforce forced tunneling (which is explained later).

> **MORE INFO**   To learn more about Network Security Groups, read the article "What is a Network Security Group (NSG)?" at *https://azure.microsoft.com/documentation/articles/virtual-networks-nsg*.

Routing tables

In the early days of Azure, some might have been a bit confused by the rationale of allowing customers to subnet their Azure Virtual Networks. The question was "What's the point of subnetting, if there's no way to exercise access controls or control routing between the subnets?" At that time, it seemed that the Azure Virtual Network, no matter how large the address block you chose and how many subnets you defined, was just a large flat network that defied the rules of TCP/IP networking.

Of course, the reason for that was because no documentation existed regarding what is known as "default system routes." When you create an Azure Virtual Network and then define subnets within it, Azure automatically creates a collection of system routes that allows machines on the various subnets you've created to communicate with each other. You don't have to define the routes, and the appropriate gateway addresses are automatically assigned by the DHCP server–provided addresses.

Default system routes allow Azure VMs to communicate across a variety of scenarios, such as:

- Communicating between subnets.
- Communicating with devices on the Internet.
- Communicating with VMs that are located on a different Azure Virtual Network (when those Azure Virtual Networks are connected to each other over a site-to-site VPN running over the Azure fabric).
- Communicating with resources on your on-premises network, either over a site-to-site VPN or over a dedicated WAN link (these options are explained later in the chapter).

That said, sometimes you might not want to use all of the default routes. This might be the case in two scenarios:

- You have a virtual network security device on an Azure Virtual Network and you want to pump all traffic through that device. (Virtual network security devices are explained later in the chapter.)
- You want to make sure that VMs on your Azure Virtual Network cannot initiate outbound connections to the Internet.

In the first scenario, you might have a virtual network security device in place that all traffic must go through so that it can be inspected. This might be a virtual IDS/IPS, a virtual firewall, a web proxy, or a data leakage protection device. Regardless of the specific function, you need to make sure that all traffic goes through it.

In the second scenario, you should ensure that VMs cannot initiate connections to the Internet. This is different from allowing VMs to respond to inbound requests from the Internet. (Of course, you have to configure a Network Security Group to allow those connections.) Also ensure that all outbound connections to the Internet that are initiated by the VMs go back through your on-premises network and out your on-premises network security devices, such as firewalls or web proxies.

The solution for both of these problems is to take advantage of User Defined Routes. In Azure, you can use User Defined Routes to control the entries in the routing table and override the default settings.

For a virtual network security device, you configure the Azure routing table to forward all outbound and inbound connections through that device. When you want to prevent VMs from initiating outbound connections to the Internet, you configure forced tunneling.

> **MORE INFO** For more information about User Defined Routes, read the article "What are User Defined Routes and IP Forwarding?" at *https://azure.microsoft.com/documentation/articles /virtual-networks-udr-overview*. For more information about forced tunneling, read "Configure forced tunneling using the Azure Resource Manager deployment model" at *https://azure.microsoft.com/documentation/articles/vpn-gateway-forced-tunneling-rm*.

Remote access (Azure gateway/point-to-site VPN/RDP/ Remote PowerShell/SSH)

One big difference between on-premises computing and public cloud computing is that in public cloud computing you don't have the same level of access to the VMs as you do on-premises. When you run your own virtualization infrastructure, you can directly access the VMs over the virtual machine bus (VMbus). Access through the VMbus takes advantage of hooks in the virtual platform to the VM so that you don't need to go over the virtual networking infrastructure.

This isn't to say that accessing a virtual machine over the VMbus is easy to achieve. There are strong access controls over VMbus access, just as you would have for any network-level access. The difference is that VMbus access for on-premises (and cloud) virtualization platforms is tightly controlled and limited to administrators of the platform. Owners of the virtual machines or the services that run on the virtual machines typically aren't allowed access over the VMbus—and if they are, this level of access is often temporary and can be revoked any time the virtualization administrators decide it's necessary.

When you have VMs on a cloud service provider's network, you're no longer the administrator of the virtualization platform. This means you no longer have direct virtual machine access over the virtualization platform's VMbus. The end result is that to reach the virtual machine for configuration and management, you need to do it over a network connection.

In addition to needing to go over a network connection, you should use a remote network connection. This might be over the Internet or over a dedicated WAN link. Cross-premises connectivity options (so-called "hybrid network connections") are explained in the next topic. This section focuses on remote access connections that you use over the Internet for the express purpose of managing VMs and the services running on the VMs.

Your options are:

- Remote Desktop Protocol (RDP)
- Secure Shell Protocol (SSH)
- Secure Socket Tunneling Protocol (SSTP)–based point-to-site VPN

Each of these methods of remote access depends on the Azure Virtual Network Gateway. This gateway can be considered the primary ingress point from the Internet into your Azure Virtual Network.

Remote Desktop Protocol

One of the easiest ways to gain remote access to a VM on an Azure Virtual Network is to use the Remote Desktop Protocol (RDP). RDP allows you to access the desktop interface of a VM on an Azure Virtual Network in the same way it does on any on-premises network. It is simple to create a Network Security Group rule that allows inbound access from the Internet to a VM by using RDP.

What's important to be aware of is that when you allow RDP to access a VM from over the Internet, you're allowing direct connections to an individual VM. No authentication gateways or proxies are in the path—you connect to a VM.

Like all simple things, using RDP might not be the best option for secure remote access to VMs. The reason for this is that RDP ports are often found to be under constant attack. Attackers typically try to use brute force to get credentials in an attempt to log onto VMs on Azure Virtual Networks. Although brute-force attacks can be slowed down and mitigated by complex user names and passwords, in many cases, VMs that are not compromised are considered temporary VMs and therefore do not have complex user names and passwords.

You might think that if these are temporary VMs, no loss or risk is involved with them being compromised. The problem with this is that sometimes customers put these temporary VMs on Azure Virtual Networks that have development VMs, or even production VMs, on them. Compromising these temporary VMs provides an attacker with an initial foothold into your deployment from which they can expand their breach. You don't want that to happen.

RDP is easy, and if you're sure that you're just testing the services and the VMs in the service, and you have no plans to do anything significant with them, then this scenario is reasonable. As you move from pure testing into something more serious, you should look at other ways to reach your VMs over the Internet. Other methods are described later in this chapter.

> **MORE INFO**   For more information about more secure remote access that uses RDP and other protocols, read the article "Securing Remote Access to Azure Virtual Machines over the Internet" at *https://blogs.msdn.microsoft.com/azuresecurity/2015/09/08 /securing-remote-access-to-azure-virtual-machines-over-the-internet*.

Secure Shell Protocol

Remote Desktop Protocol and the Secure Shell Protocol (SSH) are similar in the following ways:

- Both can be used to access both Windows and Linux VMs that are placed on an Azure Virtual Network.
- Both provide for direct connectivity to individual VMs.
- User names and passwords can be accessed by brute force.

As with RDP, you should avoid brute-force attacks. Therefore, as a best practice, you should limit direct access to VMs by using SSH over the Internet. An explanation of how you can use SSH more securely is provided in the next section.

> **MORE INFO**   For more information about how to use SSH for remote management of VMs located on an Azure Virtual Network, read the article "How to Use SSH with Linux and Mac on Azure" at *https://azure.microsoft.com/documentation/articles /virtual-machines-linux-ssh-from-linux*.

SSTP-based point-to-site VPN

Although "point-to-site" VPN in relation to Azure might sound like a new VPN-type technology (sort of like how so-called "SSL-VPN" is not really a VPN in many cases), it's not new. Rather, it's a new name applied to traditional remote access VPN client/server connections, which has been around a long time. What makes point-to-site VPN special is the VPN protocol that's used, which is the Secure Socket Tunneling Protocol (SSTP).

The SSTP VPN protocol is interesting because, unlike other methods of remote access VPN client/server connections (such as IPsec, LTP/IPsec, or PPTP), the SSTP protocol tunnels communications over the Internet by using a TLS-encrypted HTTP header. What this means in practice is that SSTP can be used across firewalls and web proxies. Some people might find it funny to hear someone say that SSTP can be used to get across "restrictive firewalls" because it uses TCP 443 to connect to the VPN gateway server from your Azure Virtual Network. It sounds funny because, among network security and firewall experts, TCP port 443 is known as the "universal firewall port." That is to say, if you allow outbound TCP 443, you allow just about everything.

For those of you who are not networking experts, you should understand what a remote access VPN client/server connection is and how it works (from a high level).

When you establish a VPN connection, what you're doing is creating a virtual "link layer" connection. (Think of an Ethernet cable connection as a link-layer connection.) The amazing thing about VPN is that this link-layer connection actually happens over the Internet and you can use it to establish that connection with a VPN server. In the case of Azure, you're establishing that connection between your laptop and the Azure gateway.

The link-layer connection is like a virtual cable (referred to in this book as a "tunnel") and you can pass just about any kind of network traffic through that tunnel. This is useful because the tunnel is encrypted, so no one can see inside the tunnel because the traffic inside the tunnel moves over the Internet.

After the VPN connection is established between your laptop and the Azure VPN gateway, your laptop isn't connected to a specific Azure VM. Instead, your laptop is connected to an entire Azure Virtual Network, and with this connection, you can reach all the VMs on that Azure Virtual Network. This helps you make RDP and SSH connections more secure. But how does it do that?

The key here is that in order to establish the point-to-site VPN connection, you have to authenticate with the VPN gateway. The Azure VPN gateway and VPN client both use certificates to authenticate with each other. Certificate authentication isn't susceptible to brute-force attacks like direct RDP or SSH connections over the Internet can be. This is a nice security advantage.

The big advantage comes from the fact that you can run RDP or SSH traffic inside the SSTP VPN tunnel. After you establish the point-to-site VPN connection, you can start your RDP or SSH client application on your laptop and connect to the IP address of the VM on the Azure Virtual Network that you're connected to. Of course, you have to authenticate again to access the VM.

This means that you can block direct inbound access for the RDP and SSH protocols to VMs on your Azure Virtual Network over the Internet and still reach them by using those protocols after you establish the VPN connection. This entire process is secure because you have to authenticate the VPN connection first, and then authenticate again with the RDP or SSH protocols.

> **MORE INFO** To learn more about point-to-site connectivity between individual computers such as laptops and tablets, read the article "Configure a Point-to-Site VPN connection to a VNet using the classic portal" at *https://azure.microsoft.com/documentation/articles /vpn-gateway-point-to-site-create*.

Cross-premises connectivity

The previous section explained how you can connect a single device like a laptop or tablet to an Azure Virtual Network to gain network access to all the VMs connected to that Azure Virtual Network. This section explains how you can connect an entire network to an Azure Virtual Network.

This introduces the topic of what is known as "cross-premises connectivity." Probably a better term would be "across sites" connectivity, but that doesn't sound as fancy. Regardless, what this term means is connectivity between two sites. The first site is usually your on-premises network (which is a network that your organization owns and controls) and an Azure Virtual Network. When cross-premises connectivity is enabled, you can pass traffic between the on-premises network and your Azure Virtual Network.

You can do this in two ways with Azure:

- Site-to-site VPN
- Dedicated WAN link

Site-to-site VPN

Site-to-site VPN is similar to the point-to-site VPN described earlier. Recall that with a point-to-site VPN, you can connect a single device (at a time) to an Azure Virtual Network. To be clear, that doesn't mean that when you use a point-to-site VPN you can only connect a single device at a time, which would block all other connections to the Azure Virtual Network. What it means is that when you use a point-to-site VPN, only that device is connected to the Azure Virtual Network. Other devices can connect to the same Azure Virtual Network by using a point-to-site VPN at the same time.

In contrast to a point-to-site VPN, with a site-to-site VPN, you can connect an entire network to an Azure Virtual Network. Site-to-site VPNs are sometimes called "gateway-to-gateway" VPNs because each end of the connection is a VPN gateway device.

VPN gateways are like routers. On a non-VPN network, a router is used to route packets to different subnets on your on-premises network. The routed connections go over Ethernet or wireless connections. A VPN gateway acts as a router too, but in the case of the VPN gateway, connections routed over the VPN gateway are not routed from one subnet to another subnet on your on-premises network. Instead, they are routed from your on-premises network to another network over the Internet by using a VPN tunnel. Of course, the remote network can also route packets back to your on-premises network.

When you use a site-to-site VPN with an Azure Virtual Network, you route packets to and from the Azure Virtual Network and your on-premises networks. You must have a VPN gateway on your on-premises network that works with the VPN gateway used by Azure. Most industry standard on-premises VPN gateways work with the Azure VPN gateway. Note that in contrast to the point-to-site VPN connections that use SSTP, the site-to-site VPN uses IPsec tunnel mode for the site-to-site VPN connection.

Using site-to-site VPN connections has a couple of downsides:

- Connections to Azure top out at around 200 megabits per second (Mbps).
- They, by definition, traverse the Internet, which could be a security issue.

The first issue really isn't a security problem, although it's related to performance and performance limitations, which can bleed into availability, which could lead to problems with the "A" in the confidentiality, integrity, and availability (CIA) triad of security. If you exceed your site-to-site VPN bandwidth and your users and devices can't get to what they need on your Azure Virtual Network, then you have a compromise in availability, and, hence, security issues. That is to say, you've essentially created a denial-of-service (DOS) attack on yourself because you chose a connectivity option that doesn't support your application and infrastructure requirements.

The second issue is more of a classic security problem. Any traffic that moves over the Internet will potentially be exposed to "hacking," "cracking," redirection, and other attempts to compromise the data. Although it is true that the site-to-site VPN uses a more secure IPsec tunnel that supports the latest cipher suites and modern encryption technologies, there is always the chance that if you have a dedicated attacker that wants your information, he will find weaknesses and compromise the data within the tunnel.

That said, if the attacker wants your data that much, he can find easier ways to get to it than to try and compromise your site-to-site VPN connection. But the possibility should be mentioned because the topic of this chapter and book is network security.

For environments that need the highest level of security and performance, you should review the option discussed in the next section, a dedicated WAN link.

> **MORE INFO** For more information about site-to-site VPN connectivity to Azure, read the article "Create a virtual network with a Site-to-Site VPN connection using the Azure classic portal" at *https://azure.microsoft.com/en-us/documentation/articles/vpn-gateway-site-to-site-create*.

Dedicated WAN link

A dedicated WAN link is a permanent connection between your on-premises network and another network. With Azure Virtual Network, a dedicated WAN link provides a permanent connection between your on-premises network and an Azure Virtual Network. These dedicated WAN links are provided by telco providers and do not traverse the Internet. These connections are private, physical connections between your network and an Azure Virtual Network.

Microsoft provides you with the option to create a dedicated WAN link between your on-premises network and Azure Virtual Network by using ExpressRoute. (The name might change over time, so be sure to check the Azure Security Team blog on a regular basis.)

ExpressRoute provides you with:

- Up to 10 gigabits per second (Gbps) of connectivity between your on-premises network and an Azure Virtual Network.
- A dedicated, private connection that does not traverse the Internet.
- A service-level agreement (SLA) that guarantees uptime and performance.

As you can see, the level of performance you get with an ExpressRoute dedicated WAN link far exceeds what you get from a site-to-site VPN. That 10 Gbps is 50 times the maximum speed available with any site-to-site VPN you can establish to an Azure Virtual Network.

The security advantage is clear: the connection doesn't traverse the Internet and therefore isn't exposed to all the potential risks that are inherent in an Internet connection. Sure, someone might be able to gain access to the telco, but the odds of that happening are much lower than the security risks that you're exposed to on the Internet.

The SLAs are important. With a site-to-site VPN, you're depending on the Internet. The Internet doesn't have SLAs, and you get the best possible effort from all the telco providers and the network they manage. Your packets move over a number of networks and you hope for the best, but in no way can anyone guarantee you uptime or performance. That's how the Internet-at-large works.

With dedicated WAN links, the telco providers control the entire network. From your premises or co-location, the telco controls all traffic and performance across the channel. They can identify where problems are and fix them, and they can improve performance anywhere they want in the path. That's why dedicated WAN links are so efficient and expensive.

Note that ExpressRoute provides two different types of dedicated WAN links:

- Multiprotocol line switching (MPLS) to your on-premises network
- Exchange Provider connectivity, where the ExpressRoute connection terminates at a Telco Exchange Provider location

The MPLS version of ExpressRoute tops out at around 1 Gbps, whereas the Exchange Provider option provides you with up to 10 Gbps.

Network availability

As explained earlier, the "A" in the CIA security triad is availability. From a network perspective, you should ensure that your services are always available and that you take advantage of network availability technologies. Azure has a few availability services that you can take advantage of:

- External load balancing
- Internal load balancing
- Global load balancing

External load balancing

To understand external load balancing, imagine that you have a three-tier application: a web front end, an application logic middle tier, and a database back end. The web front-end servers accept incoming connections from the Internet. Because the web front-end servers are state-less servers (that is to say, no information is stored on the servers that needs to persist beyond sessions), you deploy several of them. It doesn't matter which of these your users connect to, because they are all the same and they all forward connections to the middle-tier application logic servers.

To get the highest level of availability and performance from the web front-end server, you should ensure that all the incoming connections are equally distributed to each of the web front ends. You should avoid a situation where one server gets too much traffic. This kind of situation decreases application performance and possibly could make the application unavailable if that server becomes unavailable. To solve this problem, you can use external load balancing.

When you use external load balancing, incoming Internet connections are distributed among your VMs. For web front-end servers, external load balancing ensures that connections from your users are evenly distributed among those servers. This improves performance because no VM is handling an excessive load, and also improves uptime because if for some reason one or more VMs fail, other VMs you've configured the connections to be load balanced to are able to accept the connections.

Internal load balancing

External load balancing is used for incoming connections from the Internet. If you refer back to the example three-tier application discussed earlier, you might want to load balance the other tiers in the solution. The application logic tier and the database tiers are different from the web front ends because they are not Internet facing. These tiers do not allow incoming connections to the Internet. In fact, it's likely that you'll configure them so that these other tiers are only allowed to communicate with VMs that they must communicate with.

For example, the application logic tier needs to accept incoming connections from the web front ends, and no other service (for the time being, ignore the discussion about management access). In this case, you configure a Network Security Group so that the application logic tier VMs can accept only incoming connections from the web front-end servers.

Similarly, the database tier VMs do not need to accept connections from the Internet or the web front ends; they need to accept incoming connections from the application logic VMs only. In this case, you configure a Network Security Group in such a way as to allow only incoming connections from an application logic tier.

That handles the connection security part of the puzzle, but you still have the availability component to deal with. The web front ends have external load balancing to help them out with that. But what about the application logic and database servers?

For these VMs, you should use internal load balancing.

Internal load balancing works the same way as external load balancing, with the difference being that the source and destination VMs are internal; no source or destination devices are on the Internet for internal load balancing. The source and destination can all be on Azure Virtual Networks, or on an Azure Virtual Network and an on-premises network.

> **MORE INFO**   To learn more about internal load balancing, read the article "Internal Load Balancer Overview" at *https://azure.microsoft.com/documentation/articles/load-balancer-internal-overview*.

Global load balancing

With cloud computing in Microsoft Azure, you can massively scale your applications—so much so that you can make applications available to almost anybody in the world, and each user, regardless of location, can have great performance and availability.

So far, you've read about external and internal load balancing to improve availability. Although these technologies are critical to ensuring that your applications are always online, they suffer from the same limitation: they work on a per-datacenter basis. That is to say, you can only configure internal and external load balancing among VMs located in the same datacenter.

At first you might think that's not a big problem. The Azure datacenters are large, they have a huge reserve capacity, and if one or a thousand physical servers in the Azure datacenter go down, you'll still be up and running because of the built-in redundancy in the Azure fabric.

Although that's all true, you should consider what might happen if an entire datacenter becomes unavailable, or even an entire region. It's possible that the power might go out for a datacenter or an entire region due to some kind of natural or unnatural event. If your solutions are confirmed to a single datacenter or region, you might suffer from outages.

If you want to better secure yourself against these kinds of outages, you should design your applications to take advantage of the scalability of the cloud. Azure makes it possible for you to increase the scale by placing components of your applications all over the world.

The trick is to make sure that your users can access those applications. To do this, you should take advantage of something known as a "global load balancer." Global load balancers take advantage of the Domain Name System (DNS) to ensure that:

- Users access your service by connecting to the datacenter closest to that user. (For example, if a user is in Australia, that user connects to the Australian Azure datacenter and not one in North America.)

- Users access your service by connecting to the closest alternate datacenter if the closest datacenter is offline.

- Users have the best experience with your service by accessing the datacenter that is most responsive, regardless of the location of that datacenter.

Azure provides you with a global load balancer in the form of Azure Traffic Manager. With Azure Traffic Manager, you can:

- Improve the availability and responsiveness of your applications.

- Perform maintenance tasks or upgrade your applications and have them remain online and available by having users connect to an alternate location.

- Distribute and load balance traffic for complex applications that require specific load balancing requirements.

> **MORE INFO** To learn more about Traffic Manager and how you can take advantage of all its global load balancing features, read the article "What is Traffic Manager?" at *https://azure.microsoft.com/documentation/articles/traffic-manager-overview*.

Network logging

It's standard practice to access network information from the network itself. You can do this in many ways, but typically enterprise organizations include some kind of network intrusion detection system (NIDS) inline so that all network traffic can be monitored. It's a matter of opinion regarding how valuable such devices are, given the large number of never-seen alerts that are generated, and if seen, that are never addressed.

Regardless, there is some value in having visibility at the network level. For that reason, many customers are interested in how they can get the same or similar level of visibility into network traffic on their Azure Virtual Network.

At the time this chapter was written, you can't get the same level of visibility into network traffic that you can get on-premises. Many of the on-premises devices work at the Link layer (OSI layer 2), which is not available on Azure Virtual Networks. The reason for this is that Azure Virtual Networks make use of software-defined networking and network virtualization, so the lowest level of traffic analysis you can get is at the Network layer (OSI layer 3).

It is possible to get network layer network information if you want to push all traffic through a virtual network security device. That is pretty easy to do for traffic destined to and from a particular network subnet, and the way you do it on an Azure Virtual Network is the same as you would do it on-premises: you ensure that the virtual network security device is in the path to the destination subnet by configuring the routing tables on your Azure Virtual Network. You do this by configuring User Defined Routes, which were described earlier in this chapter.

Although this is easy for inter-subnet communications, it's not easy if you want to see what's happening between two VMs on the same subnet on your Azure Virtual Network. The reason for this is that you can't easily take advantage of an intermediary virtual network security device between subnets, because the two VMs that are communicating with each other are on the same subnet. That doesn't mean it can't be done. You can install a VM on each subnet that acts as a proxy (web proxy and perhaps a SOCKS proxy). Then all communications are sent to the proxy, and the proxy forwards the connections to the destination host on the same subnet. As you can imagine, this can end up being complex and unwieldy if you have even a few subnets.

At this time, you have the ability to get some network information for traffic that moves through Network Security Groups. In particular, you can:

- Use Azure audit logs to get information about connections made through a Network Security Group.
- View which Network Security Group rules are applied to VMs and instance roles based on the MAC address.
- View how many times each Network Security Group rule was applied to deny or allow traffic.

Although this is much less than you can do on-premises, the situation will most likely change soon. In fact, by the time you read this chapter, you might be able to obtain network information and bring your level of access much closer to what you have on-premises. Be sure to check the Azure Security Blog on a regular basis, where that information will be shared with you when it becomes available.

> **MORE INFO** To learn more about how you can obtain logging information from Network Security Groups, read the article "Log Analytics for Network Security Groups (NSGs)" at *https://azure.microsoft.com/documentation/articles/virtual-network-nsg-manage-log*.

Public name resolution

Although the Azure DNS service is not strictly a security offering and it doesn't necessarily connect to any specific security scenario, you should be aware that Azure has a DNS server.

You can configure DNS zones in Azure DNS. However, Azure does not provide DNS registrar services, so you'll need to register your DNS domain name with a commercial domain registrar.

> **MORE INFO**   To learn more about the Azure DNS service, read the article "Azure DNS Overview" at *https://azure.microsoft.com/documentation/articles/dns-overview*.

Network security appliances

You've read about the option to use virtual network security appliances in a number of places in this chapter. A virtual network security appliance is a VM that you can obtain from the Azure Marketplace and is usually provided by an Azure partner. These VMs are similar or the same as the network security device VMs you might be using on-premises today. Most of the major network security appliance vendors have their offerings in the Azure Marketplace today, and new ones are added daily. If you don't find what you want today, be sure to check tomorrow.

> **MORE INFO**   To learn more about what virtual network security devices are available in the Azure Marketplace, on the Azure Marketplace home page (*https://azure.microsoft.com/en-us /marketplace*), enter **security** in the search box. You can find Azure security partners at *https://azure.microsoft.com/marketplace/?term=security*.

Reverse proxy

The final Azure Network component to cover before moving on to the Azure network security best practices section is that of a reverse proxy. If you are relatively new to networking, or haven't delved into networking beyond what you needed to know, you might not be familiar with the concept of proxy or reverse proxy.

A proxy is a network device that accepts connections for other devices and then recreates that connection to forward the connection request and subsequent packets to the destination. The proxy device, as the name implies, acts on behalf of the computer that is sending the request or the response. The proxy sits in the middle of the communications channel and, because of that, can do many security-related "things" that can help secure your network and the devices within it.

The most popular type of proxy is the "web proxy." A web proxy accepts connections from a web proxy client (typically a browser configured to use the IP address of the web proxy as its web proxy). When the web proxy receives the request, it can inspect the nature of the request and then recreate the request on behalf of the web proxy client. When the destination website responds, the web proxy receives the response on behalf of the web proxy client, and it can inspect the response. After receiving the response, the web proxy client forwards the response traffic back to the client that made the original request.

Why are proxy devices useful in a security context? Some of the things they can do include the following:

- Require the requestor to authenticate before the proxy accepts and forwards the connection request.

- Inspect the destination URL to determine whether the destination is safe or dangerous; if it's dangerous, the proxy can block the connection.

- Look at request and response traffic to determine whether there is dangerous payload, such as viruses or other malware, and block the malware from being delivered.

- "Crack open" encrypted communications between client and destination server (such as SSL connections) so that malware, leaked data, and other information that shouldn't be crossing the proxy boundary is stopped at the proxy. This type of "SSL bridging" can significantly improve security, because attackers often hide what they're trying to accomplish by encrypting communications, which normally works because most communications are not subject to SSL bridging.

Proxy devices can do these things and a lot more. One could write a book about just proxies. But this book and chapter aren't about proxies, so don't dig deeper into them than necessary.

The reason to bring up proxies in this chapter is that Azure has a reverse proxy service that you can use to proxy connections to your on-premises resources. The reverse proxy service is called Azure Active Directory Application Proxy. You won't find this service in the list of Azure Active Directory products on *Azure.com*, and you won't find it in the table of contents. However, you'll learn about it in this book.

Before going any further, it's important that you understand the difference between a "forward proxy" and a "reverse proxy." A forward proxy accepts connections from clients on your on-premises network and forwards those connections to servers on the Internet (or on networks other than the one on which the clients are making the requests). In contrast, a reverse proxy is one that accepts connections from external clients and forwards them to servers on your on-premises network. For those of you with a lot of experience in this area, you recognize that this is a bit of an oversimplification, but it does describe in general the differences between a forward and reverse proxy.

Traditional reverse proxy devices are typically placed near the edge of your on-premises network. Servers such as mail servers and collaboration servers (like Microsoft Exchange and SharePoint) can be reached by Internet-based clients through the reverse proxy server. Microsoft used to have its own reverse proxy servers named Internet Security and Acceleration Server

(ISA Server) and Threat Management Gateway (TMG). Both those products were excellent but unfortunately were discontinued.

With that said, maintaining on-premises proxy servers can be a lot of work. If you don't manage them well, they can take down your services, which makes no one happy. What if you could hand the management, troubleshooting, and updating of your reverse proxy server to someone else and avoid all that hassle?

That's the core value of the public cloud, and the core value of using the Azure Application Proxy server instead of using an on-premises reverse proxy.

The Azure Application Proxy is already built into Azure, and you configure it so that when client systems want to request resources on your on-premises servers, they actually make the request to the reverse proxy on Azure. The Azure Application Proxy forwards those requests back to your on-premises servers.

Like most reverse proxy solutions, they add a measure of security. Here are some things you can do with the Azure Application reverse proxy service:

- Enable single sign-on for on-premises applications.
- Enforce conditional access, which helps you to define whether or not a user can access the application based on the user's current location (on or off the corporate network).
- Authenticate users before their connections are forwarded to the Azure Application Proxy.

> **MORE INFO** To learn more about the Azure Application Proxy, read the article "Publish applications using Azure AD Application Proxy" at *https://azure.microsoft.com/documentation/articles/active-directory-application-proxy-publish*.

Azure Network Security best practices

At this point, you should have a good understanding of what Azure has to offer in the network security space. This chapter provided information about all the major components of Azure networking that have some kind of tie to security, and went over a number of examples so that you have context for each of the components. If you remember and understand everything you've read so far, consider yourself in the top 10 percent of the class when it comes to Azure networking.

Although understanding the various aspects of Azure networking is required to ensure that your deployments are secure, knowing what those aspects are and how they work is the first step. What you should do now is put that knowledge into action by learning a few best practices.

About best practices

The best practices I describe in this section are based on my 20-year experience with network security in general and my 5-year experience with Azure networking in particular. Of course, best practices are based on two things: the positive experience others have had using a specific practice and the confirmation that the best practices work across a number of environments. Understanding this is key, because it's important for you to understand that I didn't come up with these best practices on my own—I've learned from our customers, from the Microsoft field, and from the engineers who created the Azure networking technologies. Thus, these best practices represent an amalgam of multiple groups of people who are smarter than me—and now I'm sharing with you the results of my experiences.

Tom Shinder
Program Manager, Azure Security Engineering

One more thing about best practices: one size does not fit all. Although these best practices are good things to do in most cases, they aren't good things to do in all cases. You always have to consider the environment in which you're considering these best practices. Sometimes you won't need to use one of these best practices because they just don't apply. Use your best judgment and do what is best for your network.

This section covers the following Azure networking best practices:

- Subnet your networks based on security zones.
- Use Network Security Groups carefully.
- Use site-to-site VPN to connect Azure Virtual Networks.
- Configure host-based firewalls on infrastructure as a service (IaaS) virtual machines.
- Configure User Defined Routes to control traffic.
- Require forced tunneling.
- Deploy virtual network security appliances.
- Create perimeter networks for Internet-facing devices.
- Use ExpressRoute.
- Optimize uptime and performance.
- Disable management protocols to virtual machines.
- Enable Azure Security Center.
- Extend your datacenter into Azure.

Subnet your networks based on security zones

As mentioned earlier, in the section about Azure Virtual Networks, when you create a new Azure Virtual Network, you're asked to select an IP address space in the Class A, B, or C range. These Azure Virtual Network IP address ranges are large, so you should always create multiple subnets. This is no different than what you do on-premises today.

One thing you should think about is what IP address space you want to use on your Azure Virtual Network. If you plan to connect your on-premises network to one or more Azure Virtual Networks, you need to ensure that there are no IP address conflicts. That is to say, you have to ensure that the IP address ranges you select and the subnets you create on your Azure Virtual Networks do not overlap with what you have on-premises. If there is overlap, that would cause routing table conflicts, and traffic will not be routed correctly to your subnets on your Azure Virtual Networks.

After you decide on your IP address range for your Azure Virtual Network, the next step is deciding how you want to define your subnets. One approach is to define your subnets based on the roles of the VMs you intend to place on those subnets.

For example, suppose you have the following classes of services you want to deploy on an Azure Virtual Network:

- **Active Directory Domain Controllers** You want these to support domain-joined VMs on your Azure Virtual Network.
- **Web front-end servers** You use these to support your three-tier applications.
- **Application logic servers** You use these to support middleware functions for your three-tier applications.
- **Database servers** You use these as the database back ends for your three-tier applications.
- **Update servers** You use these servers to centralize operating system and application updates for the VMs on your Azure Virtual Network.
- **DNS servers** You use these to support Active Directory and non–Active Directory name resolution for servers on your Azure Virtual Network.

You could create just one big subnet and put all your VMs on the same subnet. However, that's not a great way to help you enable secure network access control. A better solution is to define subnets for each of these roles and then put each VM that supports these roles into a subnet created for each role. That leads you to putting the domain controllers on the domain controllers' subnet, the database servers on the database server subnet, the web front ends on the web front-ends subnet, and so on.

Not only does this help you keep track of where the various servers that participate in each role are located, it also makes it much easier to manage network access controls. For example, if you choose to use NSGs for network access control, you can create a set of rules that is appropriate for all the VMs on the particular subnet. If you need to put another VM on one of the subnets, you don't need to update the NSG rules, because the existing rules will support all the machines on the subnet because they perform the same roles.

To make this clearer, consider the following simple situation with two subnets:

- Web front-end subnet
- Application logic subnet

Only web front-end VMs go into the web front-end subnet, and only application logic VMs go into the application logic subnet.

The rules for the web front-end subnet might look like this:

- Allow inbound TCP port 443 from the Internet to all IP addresses on the web front-end subnet.
- Allow outbound TCP port 443 from the web front-end subnet to all IP addresses in the application logic server's subnet.

The rules for the application logic server subnet might look like this:

- Allow inbound TCP port 443 from the web front-end subnet to all IP addresses on the application logic server's subnet.
- Allow outbound TCP port 1433 from the application logic server's subnet to all IP addresses on the database server subnet.

With these basic rules in place, you can easily put more front-end web servers onto the front-end web server's subnet without having to make any changes in the Network Security Group rules. The same goes with the application logic server's subnet.

Use Network Security Groups carefully

Although Network Security Groups are useful for basic network access control, keep in mind that they do not provide you any level of application layer inspection. All you have control over is the source and destination IP address, source and destination TCP or UDP port number, and the direction to allow access.

Another thing to be aware of is that if you want to create restrictive access rules with Network Security Groups, you have to be aware of what you might inadvertently block. Here are a few examples:

- VMs need to be able to communicate with IP addresses specific to the host operating system to get DHCP information. If you block access to this host port (which you need to discover by checking an ipconfig on your VMs to see what IP address is being used by the DHCP server), then your VMs will not be able to communicate with the DHCP server and will not be assigned IP addressing information.

- The DHCP server not only assigns an IP address to the VMs; it also assigns a DNS server and a default gateway. The DNS server will be a host server IP address (that is to say, an IP address owned by the host server, not by you), and the default gateway will be an address on your Azure Virtual Network subnet. If you block access to these IP addresses, you won't be able to perform name resolution or reach remote subnets. Neither of these conditions leads to trouble-free performance.

- Another scenario you might not think of is communications outside of your Azure Virtual Network, but still within the Azure fabric itself; for example, when you encrypt Azure Virtual Machines by using Azure Disk Encryption. To encrypt your operating system and data disks, the VM needs to be able to reach the Azure Key Vault Service and an Azure Application (these are prerequisites for Azure Disk Encryption). If you lock down your NSGs too tight, you won't be able to reach the Key Vault or the Azure Active Directory application, and your VMs won't start because the disks can't be unencrypted.

These are just a few examples. The message is to test your NSG rules thoroughly before going into production. By thoroughly testing, you won't have to deal with nasty surprises that might turn a successful deployment into a painful experience.

Use site-to-site VPN to connect Azure Virtual Networks

Eventually, you might decide you want to move the majority of your on-premises services into the Azure public cloud. You are likely going to find that as your presence in Azure grows, so will your need to use multiple Azure Virtual Networks.

You might want more than one Azure Virtual Network for many reasons. Some examples include:

- You have multiple on-premises datacenters and you want to connect to Azure Virtual Networks that are closest to the datacenter.

- You want resources in one region to be able to communicate with resources in another region over the fastest route possible.

> **NOTE** Communications over the Azure fabric are faster than looping back through your on-premises network or looping through the Internet.

- You want to use different Azure Virtual Networks to manage different classes of services, or assign them to different departments, or even different divisions or subsidiaries within your company.

These are just three examples, but you can probably come up with more. The point is that Azure Virtual Networks can grow as quickly as your on-premises network has over time. And at some point, you're going to want to connect some of those Azure Virtual Networks to one another.

The best way to do this is to connect them to each other over a site-to-site VPN connection over the Azure fabric. The site-to-site connection between the Azure Virtual Networks is similar to the site-to-site connection you establish between your on-premises network and an Azure Virtual Network. The difference is that the entire communications path between the Azure Virtual Networks is contained within the highly optimized Azure fabric itself.

An alternative to this approach is to have the Azure Virtual Networks communicate with each other over the Internet. This approach has security and performance implications that make it inferior to site-to-site VPN over the Azure fabric. Another alternative is to loop back through your on-premises network and out through another gateway on your network. In most cases, this is also a less efficient and potentially less secure solution.

> **MORE INFO** For more information about how to create a site-to-site VPN connection between two Azure Virtual Networks, read the article "Configure a VNet-to-VNet Connection by using Azure Resource Manager and PowerShell" at *https://azure.microsoft.com/documentation/articles /vpn-gateway-vnet-vnet-rm-ps*.

Configure host-based firewalls on IaaS virtual machines

This is a best practice on-premises and in the cloud. Regardless of what operating system you deploy in Azure Virtual Machines, you want to make sure that a host-based firewall is enabled, just as you do on-premises.

Another feature of the host-based firewall on Windows virtual machines is IPsec. Although IPsec for intranet communications isn't widely used, there's always a good reason to turn on IPsec—that reason being that no network can be trusted and, therefore, regardless of where that network is and who owns and operates it, you should always consider any network (wired and wireless) untrusted and untrustable.

The dichotomy of the "trusted corporate network" versus "untrusted non-corporate networks" sounded good in the past before the widespread use of the Internet. But with the collision of multiple trends, such as cloud computing, using your own device, multi-homed devices (wireless devices that connect to a corporate network and other wireless networks at the same time), and numerous portable storage devices of all shapes, sizes, and capacities, it's not realistic to think that there is a material difference between the innate security of your on-premises network and any other network, including the Internet.

Well, there might be, but to think and act otherwise puts you at more risk than you need to be. That's why you should use IPsec for all communications that aren't encrypted by some other method (such as HTTPS or encrypted SMB 3.0). You can use IPsec on Azure Virtual Network to authenticate and encrypt all wire communications between VMs on the Azure Virtual Network, in addition to communications between those VMs in Azure and any devices you have on-premises.

If you do choose to use IPsec, be careful not to block host ports responsible for DHCP and DNS resolution, in addition to the default gateway and any storage addresses your VM might need access to.

> **MORE INFO** To learn more about how to use IPsec for server and domain isolation, read the article "Server and Domain Isolation Using IPsec and Group Policy" at *https://technet.microsoft.com /library/cc163159.aspx*.

Configure User Defined Routes to control traffic

When you put a VM on an Azure Virtual Network, you might notice that the VM can connect to any other VM on the same Azure Virtual Network, even if the other VMs are on different subnets. This is possible because there is a collection of system routes that are enabled by default that allow this type of communication. These default routes allow VMs on the same Azure Virtual Network to initiate connections with each other, and with the Internet (for outbound communications to the Internet only).

Although the default system routes are useful for many deployment scenarios, sometimes you might want to customize the routing configuration for your deployments. These customizations allow you to configure the next hop address to reach specific destinations.

You should configure User Defined Routes when you deploy a virtual network security appliance, which is described in a later best practice.

There are other scenarios where you might want to configure custom routes. For example, you might have multiple network security appliances that you want to forward traffic to on the same or other Azure Virtual Networks. You might even have multiple gateways you want to use, such as a scenario where you have a cross-premises connection between your Azure Virtual Network and your on-premises location, in addition to a site-to-site VPN that connects your Azure Virtual Network to another Azure Virtual Network or even multiple Azure Virtual Networks.

Just as in the on-premises world, you might end up requiring a complex routing infrastructure to support your network security requirements. For this reason, paying close attention to your User Defined Routes will significantly improve your overall network security. Of course, ensure that you document all your customizations and include the rationale behind each one you make.

> **MORE INFO** To learn more about User Defined Routes, read the article "What are User Defined Routes and IP Forwarding" at *https://azure.microsoft.com/documentation/articles /virtual-networks-udr-overview*.

Require forced tunneling

If you haven't spent a lot of time in the networking space, the term "forced tunneling" might sound a little odd. In the context of Azure networking, it can sound odd even to those who have experience in networking.

To understand why the term might sound odd, it helps to understand where the term comes from. First, what is "tunneling"? As explained earlier in this chapter when we covered VPN technologies, tunneling is a way to move data through an encrypted channel. (For you network purists out there, yes, you can tunnel within non-encrypted protocols, but let's keep it simple here.) When you establish a VPN connection, you create an encrypted tunnel between two network devices. After the tunnel is established, information can travel more securely within that tunnel.

Now consider a common scenario that many have experienced. You're at a hotel room and need to create a VPN connection between your laptop and the VPN server at your company. You use whatever software you need to use to establish the VPN connection. After you establish the connection, you can access servers and services on the corporate network as though you are directly connected to the corporate network.

Let's say that you want to go to a non-corporate website. You open your browser, enter the address, and go to the site. Does that connection go over the VPN connection and out your corporate firewalls, and then back through your corporate firewalls and back to your laptop over the VPN connection for the response?

It depends.

If your computer is configured to allow split-tunneling when using the VPN connection, it means that your computer will access the site by going over the Internet—it will not try to reach the site by going through your VPN connection to the corporate network and out to the Internet through your corporate network firewalls.

Most organizations consider this a security risk because when split-tunneling is enabled, your computer can essentially act as a bridge between the Internet and the corporate network, because it can access both the Internet and your corporate network at the same time. Attackers can take advantage of this "dual connection" to reach your corporate network through your split-tunneling computer.

The term "split-tunneling" itself is a bit of a misnomer, because there's only a single "tunnel" here: the encrypted VPN tunnel to your corporate network. The connection to the Internet itself is not "tunneled." So technically, you don't have a "split tunnel"; you have a "dual connection." Regardless, sometimes names for things aren't rational, so you'll have to accept the industry standard name for this phenomenon.

Let's say that you don't want to deal with the risk of split tunneling when your users are connected to your corporate network over VPN. What do you do? You configure something called "forced tunneling." When forced tunneling is configured, all traffic is forced to go over the VPN tunnel. If you want to go to a non-corporate website, then that request is going to go over the VPN connection and over your corporate network to your corporate firewalls, and then the corporate firewalls will receive the responses and forward the responses back to you over the VPN connection. There will be no "direct" connections to any Internet servers (with "direct" meaning that the connections avoid going over the VPN connection).

What does this have to do with Azure network security?

The default routes for an Azure Virtual Network allow VMs to initiate traffic to the Internet. This process can pose a security risk because it represents a form of split tunneling, and these outbound connections could increase the attack surface of a VM and be used by attackers. For this reason, you should enable forced tunneling on your VMs when you have cross-premises connectivity between your Azure Virtual Network and your on-premises network.

If you do not have a cross-premises connection, be sure to take advantage of Network Security Groups (discussed earlier) or Azure Virtual Network security appliances (discussed next) to prevent outbound connections to the Internet from your Azure Virtual Machines.

> **MORE INFO** To learn more about forced tunneling and how to enable it, read the article "Configure forced tunneling using the Azure Resource Manager deployment model" at *https://azure.microsoft.com/en-us/documentation/articles/vpn-gateway-forced-tunneling-rm*.

Deploy virtual network security appliances

Although Network Security Groups and User Defined Routes can provide a certain measure of network security at the network and transport layers of the OSI model, in some situations, you'll want or need to enable security at high levels of the stack. In such situations, you should deploy virtual network security appliances provided by Azure partners.

Azure network security appliances can deliver significantly enhanced levels of security over what is provided by network level controls. Some of the network security capabilities provided by virtual network security appliances include:

- Firewalling
- Intrusion detection and prevention
- Vulnerability management
- Application control
- Network-based anomaly detection
- Web filtering
- Antivirus protection
- Botnet protection

If you require a higher level of network security than you can obtain with network-level access controls, then you should investigate and deploy Azure Virtual Network security appliances.

> **MORE INFO** To learn about what Azure Virtual Network security appliances are available, and about their capabilities, visit the Azure Marketplace at *https://azure.microsoft.com/marketplace* and search on "security" and "network security."

Create perimeter networks for Internet-facing devices

A perimeter network (also known as a DMZ, demilitarized zone, or screened subnet) is a physical or logical network segment that is designed to provide an additional layer of security between your assets and the Internet. The intent of the perimeter network is to place specialized network access control devices on the edge of the perimeter network so that only the traffic you want is allowed past the network security device and into your Azure Virtual Network.

Perimeter networks are useful because you can focus your network access control management, monitoring, logging, and reporting on the devices at the edge of your Azure Virtual Network. Here you would typically enable distributed denial-of-service (DDoS) prevention, IDS and IPS, firewall rules and policies, web filtering, network antimalware, and more. The network security devices sit between the Internet and your Azure Virtual Network and have an interface on both networks.

Although this is the basic design of a perimeter network, many different perimeter network designs exist, such as back-to-back, tri-homed, and multi-homed.

For all high-security deployments, you should consider deploying a perimeter network to enhance the level of network security for your Azure resources.

> **MORE INFO**   To learn more about perimeter networks and how to deploy them in Azure, read the article "Microsoft Cloud Services and Network Security" at *https://azure.microsoft.com /documentation/articles/best-practices-network-security*.

Use ExpressRoute

Many organizations have chosen the hybrid IT route. In hybrid IT, some of the company's information assets are in Azure, while others remain on-premises. In many cases, some components of a service are running in Azure while other components remain on-premises.

In the hybrid IT scenario, there is usually some type of cross-premises connectivity. This cross-premises connectivity allows the company to connect their on-premises networks to Azure Virtual Networks. Two cross-premises connectivity solutions are available:

- Site-to-site VPN
- ExpressRoute

Site-to-site VPN represents a virtual private connection between your on-premises network and an Azure Virtual Network. This connection takes place over the Internet and allows you to "tunnel" information inside an encrypted link between your network and Azure. Site-to-site VPN is a secure, mature technology that is deployed by enterprises of all sizes. Tunnel encryption is performed by using IPsec tunnel mode.

Although site-to-site VPN is a trusted, reliable, and established technology, traffic within the tunnel does traverse the Internet. In addition, bandwidth is relatively constrained to a maximum of about 200 Mbps.

If you require an exceptional level of security or performance for your cross-premises connections, you should consider using Azure ExpressRoute for your cross-premises connectivity. ExpressRoute is a dedicated WAN link between your on-premises location or an Exchange hosting provider. Because this is a telco connection, your data doesn't travel over the Internet and therefore is not exposed to the potential risks inherent in Internet communications.

> **MORE INFO** To learn more about how Azure ExpressRoute works and how to deploy it, read the article "ExpressRoute Technical Overview" at *https://azure.microsoft.com/documentation/articles /best-practices-network-security*.

Optimize uptime and performance

Confidentiality, integrity, and availability (CIA) make up the three factors for evaluating a customer's security implementation. Confidentiality is about encryption and privacy, integrity is about making sure that data is not changed by unauthorized personnel, and availability is about making sure that authorized individuals are able to access the information they are authorized to access. Failure in any one of these areas represents a potential security breach.

Availability can be thought of as being about uptime and performance. If a service is down, information can't be accessed. If performance is so poor as to make the data unavailable, then you can consider the data to be inaccessible. Therefore, from a security perspective, you should do whatever you can to ensure that your services have optimal uptime and performance. A popular and effective method used to enhance availability and performance is to use load balancing. Load balancing is a method of distributing network traffic across servers that are part of a service. For example, if you have front-end web servers as part of your service, you can use load balancing to distribute the traffic across your multiple front-end web servers.

This distribution of traffic increases availability because if one of the web servers becomes unavailable, the load balancer will stop sending traffic to that server and redirect traffic to the servers that are still online. Load balancing also helps performance, because the processor, network, and memory overhead for serving requests is distributed across all the load balanced servers.

You should consider employing load balancing whenever you can, and as appropriate for your services. The following sections discuss appropriateness situations. At the Azure Virtual Network level, Azure provides you with three primary load balancing options:

- HTTP-based load balancing
- External load balancing
- Internal load balancing

HTTP-based load balancing

HTTP-based load balancing bases decisions about which server to send connections to by using characteristics of the HTTP protocol. Azure has an HTTP load balancer named Application Gateway.

You should consider using Azure Application Gateway when you have:

- Applications that require requests from the same user or client session to reach the same back-end VM. Examples of this are shopping cart apps and web mail servers.

- Applications that want to free web server farms from SSL termination overhead by taking advantage of Application Gateway's SSL offload feature.

- Applications, such as a content delivery network, that require multiple HTTP requests on the same long-running TCP connection to be routed or load balanced to different back-end servers.

> **MORE INFO**   To learn more about how Azure Application Gateway works and how you can use it in your deployments, read the article "Application Gateway Overview" at *https://azure.microsoft.com /documentation/articles/application-gateway-introduction*.

External load balancing

External load balancing takes place when incoming connections from the Internet are load balanced among your servers located in an Azure Virtual Network. The Azure External Load Balancer can provide you with this capability, and you should consider using it when you don't require the sticky sessions or SSL offload.

In contrast to HTTP-based load balancing, the External Load Balancer uses information at the network and transport layers of the OSI networking model to make decisions on what server to load balance connections to.

You should consider using External Load Balancing whenever you have stateless applications accepting incoming requests from the Internet.

> **MORE INFO**   To learn more about how the Azure External Load Balancer works and how you can deploy it, read the article "Get Started Creating an Internet Facing Load Balancer in Resource Manager using PowerShell" at *https://azure.microsoft.com/documentation/articles /load-balancer-get-started-internet-arm-ps*.

Internal load balancing

Internal load balancing is similar to external load balancing and uses the same mechanism to load balance connections to the servers behind them. The only difference is that the load balancer in this case is accepting connections from VMs that are not on the Internet. In most cases, the connections that are accepted for load balancing are initiated by devices on an Azure Virtual Network.

You should consider using internal load balancing for scenarios that will benefit from this capability, such as when you need to load balance connections to SQL servers or internal web servers.

Global load balancing

Public cloud computing makes it possible to deploy globally distributed applications that have components located in datacenters all over the world. This is possible on Azure due to its global datacenter presence. In contrast to the load balancing technologies mentioned earlier, global load balancing makes it possible to make services available even when entire datacenters might become unavailable.

You can get this type of global load balancing in Azure by taking advantage of Azure Traffic Manager. Traffic Manager makes it possible to load balance connections to your services based on the location of the user.

For example, if the user is making a request to your service from the European Union, the connection is directed to your services located in a European Union datacenter. This part of Traffic Manager global load balancing helps to improve performance because connecting to the nearest datacenter is faster than connecting to datacenters that are far away.

On the availability side, global load balancing ensures that your service is available even if an entire datacenter becomes available.

For example, if an Azure datacenter becomes unavailable due to environmental reasons or outages such as regional network failures, connections to your service would be rerouted to the nearest online datacenter. This global load balancing is accomplished by taking advantage of DNS policies that you can create in Traffic Manager.

You should consider using Traffic Manager for any cloud solution you develop that has a widely distributed scope across multiple regions and requires the highest level of uptime possible.

Disable management protocols to virtual machines

It is possible to reach Azure Virtual Machines by using RDP and SSH protocols. These protocols make it possible to manage VMs from remote locations and are standard in datacenter computing.

The potential security problem with using these protocols over the Internet is that attackers can use various brute-force techniques to gain access to Azure Virtual Machines. After the attackers gain access, they can use your VM as a launch point for compromising other machines on your Azure Virtual Network or even attack networked devices outside of Azure.

Because of this, you should consider disabling direct RDP and SSH access to your Azure Virtual Machines from the Internet. With direct RDP and SSH access from the Internet disabled, you have other options you can use to access these VMs for remote management:

- Point-to-site VPN
- Site-to-site VPN
- ExpressRoute

Point-to-site VPN is another term for a remote access VPN client or server connection. A point-to-site VPN enables a single user to connect to an Azure Virtual Network over the Internet. After the point-to-site connection is established, the user is able to use RDP or SSH to connect to any VMs located on the Azure Virtual Network that the user connected to via point-to-site VPN. This assumes that the user is authorized to reach those VMs.

Point-to-site VPN is more secure than direct RDP or SSH connections because the user has to authenticate twice before connecting to a VM. First, the user needs to authenticate (and be authorized) to establish the point-to-site VPN connection; second, the user needs to authenticate (and be authorized) to establish the RDP or SSH session.

A site-to-site VPN connects an entire network to another network over the Internet. You can use a site-to-site VPN to connect your on-premises network to an Azure Virtual Network. If you deploy a site-to-site VPN, users on your on-premises network are able to connect to VMs on your Azure Virtual Network by using the RDP or SSH protocol over the site-to-site VPN connection, and it does not require you to allow direct RDP or SSH access over the Internet.

You can also use a dedicated WAN link to provide functionality similar to the site-to-site VPN. The main differences are:

- The dedicated WAN link doesn't traverse the Internet.
- Dedicated WAN links are typically more stable and performant.

Azure provides you with a dedicated WAN link solution in the form of ExpressRoute.

Enable Azure Security Center

Azure Security Center helps you prevent, detect, and respond to threats, and provides you with increased visibility into, and control over, the security of your Azure resources. It provides integrated security monitoring and policy management across your Azure subscriptions, helps detect threats that might otherwise go unnoticed, and works with a broad ecosystem of security solutions.

Azure Security Center helps you optimize and monitor network security by:

- Providing network security recommendations.
- Monitoring the state of your network security configuration.
- Alerting you to network-based threats both at the endpoint and network levels.

It is highly recommended that you enable Azure Security Center for all of your Azure deployments.

> **MORE INFO**   Azure Security Center is covered in more detail in Chapter 7, "Azure resource management security."

Extend your datacenter into Azure

Many enterprise IT organizations are looking to expand into the cloud instead of growing their on-premises datacenters. This expansion represents an extension of existing IT infrastructure into the public cloud. By taking advantage of cross-premises connectivity options, it's possible to treat your Azure Virtual Network as just another subnet on your on-premises network infrastructure.

However, many planning and design issues need to be addressed first. This is especially important in the area of network security. One of the best ways to understand how you approach such a design is to see an example.

Microsoft has created the Datacenter Extension Reference Architecture Diagram and supporting collateral to help you understand what such a datacenter extension would look like. This provides a reference implementation that you can use to plan and design a secure enterprise datacenter extension to the cloud. You should review this document to get an idea of the key components of a secure solution.

> **MORE INFO** For more information about the Datacenter Extension Reference Architecture Diagram, read "Datacenter extension reference architecture diagram – Interactive" at *https://gallery.technet.microsoft.com/Datacenter-extension-687b1d84*.

## CHAPTER 4

Data and storage security

D ata and storage security are about securing the data while it is at rest. The title of the chapter might seem a bit redundant, because data and storage security can be thought of as the same thing. However, many people think of storage security as securing the disk on which the data is stored. Any security for the data itself is inherited from the security applied to the storage system. In contrast, data security is security applied directly to the data, so no matter what the storage medium is, the data remains as secure as possible. Both data and storage security can be contrasted with network security, where the data is off the disk, and data inherits whatever security characteristics are applied to the network communications.

All this is to say that this chapter is mostly about data at rest. The data could reside on a file server, in a database, in an email client, or in many other types of services or applications. The key factor is that the data isn't moving over the wire, with the exception of a wire encryption protocol that you can use to share data over the wire. Wire encryption is also discussed in this chapter.

This chapter provides insights into a variety of Microsoft Azure security–related services and technologies that are applied to data-at-rest scenarios. These include:

- Virtual machine (VM) encryption
- Storage encryption
- File share wire encryption
- Hybrid data encryption
- Rights management
- Database security

Each topic describes the feature or service, what value it brings to you, and what problems it solves. You also receive pointers to valuable resources where you can get more information on each of the subjects.

Virtual machine encryption

In the past, IT organizations ran their services on physical hardware, and in many cases, ran a single service per physical server. If you needed 20 servers running Microsoft Exchange Server, then you ran 20 physical servers. To support those Exchange Servers, you needed Domain Name System (DNS) servers, domain controllers, DHCP servers, certificate services, firewalls, database servers, and more. All of these supporting servers, in addition to the Exchange Servers, ran on physical hardware. As you can imagine, things got expensive fast.

Today, most datacenters use server virtualization technology to replace the "one service per server" situation. Now, you can virtualize all those physical servers and run them as virtualized instances on a virtualization server. The virtualization platform might be Microsoft Hyper-V, VMware, or some other virtualization platform. With server virtualization, you can run 10 to 20 or more virtualized servers on a single physical server.

IT organizations rallied behind server virtualization because it solved a major cost and facilities problem: there was no more room to put physical servers and no more money to buy them. Server virtualization was quickly adopted by IT organizations because it saved money, time, and space, and made most IT shops' lives easier.

However, regardless of how compelling and useful a technology like server virtualization can be (and is), security concerns always follow. Back in the day of the physical server, if someone wanted to steal all the disks in the physical server, that person had to gain access to the facility and then the server room, and then try to get into the server enclosures themselves. Although this could be (and has been) done, a lot of overhead and risk was involved, so stealing physical hard drives was never the top choice for attackers who wanted to access all the data on a physical disk. More often, they did that over the network.

In today's world of virtualized servers, the "server" isn't a piece of hardware; it's now a piece (or pieces) of software. The operating system disk is just a disk file. Data disks that are used by the operating system disk are also disk files. These files are like any other files and can be changed, copied, or deleted with relative ease.

The implication of this is that anyone who has access to the storage can potentially copy the VM's files to another location. The attacker who has copied these VM files can then easily mount them and view anything on the file system. Even if the storage media itself is encrypted (as with whole-volume disk encryption), when the files are removed from the volume, they no longer inherit the security from the volume that they were located on; they are now unencrypted.

To solve this problem, you need to be able to encrypt the actual virtual disk files that include your VMs. Azure has such a solution, known as Azure Disk Encryption.

Azure Disk Encryption

Azure Disk Encryption is a technology that you can use to encrypt the VM disk files for your Azure VMs. Azure uses Hyper-V as its virtualization platform, so the VMs you run on Azure use the .vhd file format. With Azure Disk Encryption, you can encrypt both the operating system .vhd and any data disk .vhd files that you have attached to your VMs.

If an attacker successfully accessed your VM disk files and copied them, the attacker would not be able to mount them, because the disks are encrypted and the attacker does not have the key required to decrypt them. This is a powerful security technology that you should always employ on any VM you run on Azure. You should also use similar technology on any VM you run on-premises.

Azure Disk Encryption works for both Windows and Linux VMs. For Windows VMs, Microsoft uses BitLocker as the disk encryption technology. For Linux VMs, Microsoft uses dm-crypt. Although the specifics of the encryption technologies are a bit different, both of these volume encryption methodologies have passed the test of time and are well-trusted in the security community.

At the time this chapter was written, Azure Disk Encryption is still in public preview except in Australia, where it is generally available. There is a good chance that the service will be generally available for almost all countries/regions by the time you read this chapter.

Azure Disk Encryption supports the following scenarios:

- You can bring a VM that you've already encrypted on-premises into Azure and use the same keys you used to encrypt that VM.

- You can create a VM from the Microsoft Azure Marketplace and encrypt that VM as you create it.

- You can have unencrypted VMs that are currently running in Azure and encrypt them.

- You can unencrypt VMs that you have encrypted, regardless of whether you've encrypted them on-premises, encrypted them from the time you created them in Azure, or encrypted them after you created them.

The location of the encryption keys is important because these keys safeguard your disks. If these keys were compromised, your VMs would be too. To help ensure the security of your keys, you can sort the keys (in the case of BitLocker) or the secrets (in the case of dm-crypt) in Azure Key Vault. Key Vault is the Azure "vaulting" solution that provides you with a hardware security module (HSM) in which you store your disk encryption keys. When you encrypt a VM by using Azure Disk Encryption, you use can use an existing Key Vault or create a new one.

Figure 4-1 provides a high-level view of Azure Disk Encryption.

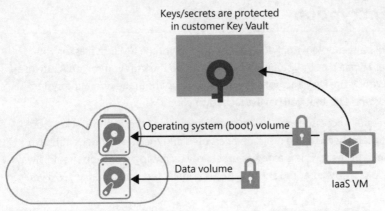

Keys/secrets are protected
in customer Key Vault

Operating system (boot) volume

Data volume

IaaS VM

FIGURE 4-1 High-level view of how Azure Disk Encryption works with Azure Key Vault

MORE INFO   To learn more about Azure Key Vault, read Chapter 6, "Key management in Azure with Key Vault."

The following lists key points you might want to know about Azure Disk Encryption:

- Currently, no charges are incurred for encrypting VMs.

- Not all operating systems can be encrypted.

- Not all operating systems can be decrypted.

- Not all types of virtual disk storage can be encrypted.

- You can use the Azure command-line interface (CLI), Azure PowerShell, or Azure Resource Manager templates to encrypt an Azure VM.

- The Azure VM and the Key Vault you use to store the VM's keys must be in the same Azure country/region.

- An Azure Active Directory application must be configured for Azure Disk Encryption usage.

- A Key Vault access policy must be configured.

MORE INFO   Note that we're not providing specific details on these key points, because they might change by the time you read this. To get detailed information, read "Azure Disk Encryption for Windows and Linux Azure Virtual Machines" at *https://gallery.technet.microsoft.com /Azure-Disk-Encryption-for-a0018eb0* or "Encrypt an Azure Virtual Machine" at *https://azure.microsoft.com/documentation/articles/security-center-disk-encryption*.

Azure Disk Encryption is also integrated into Azure Security Center. Azure Security Center is an Azure service that helps you prevent, detect, and respond to threats against your Azure resources. It provides integrated security monitoring and policy management across your Azure subscriptions, helps detect threats that might otherwise go unnoticed, and works with a broad ecosystem of security solutions. Many of the benefits of Azure Security Center are covered in Chapter 7, "Azure resource management security."

Azure Security Center alerts you if you have unencrypted VMs and categorizes unencrypted VMs as a high security risk, as shown in Figure 4-2.

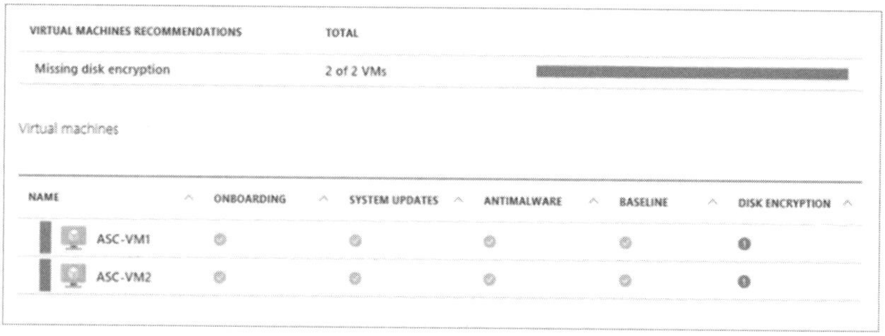

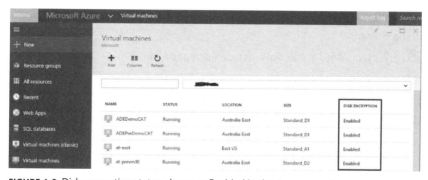

FIGURE 4-2 Azure Security Center displaying an alert for unencrypted disks

When you get such an alert, you can use Azure CLI, Azure PowerShell, or Azure Resource Manager templates to encrypt the VM. At the time of this writing, you can't remediate this alert from within the Azure Security Center console.

> **MORE INFO**   If you are proficient in CLI, PowerShell, or Azure Resource Manager templates, you'll find the information you need to know to encrypt VMs in the articles "Azure Disk Encryption for Windows and Linux Azure Virtual Machines" at *https://gallery.technet.microsoft.com /Azure-Disk-Encryption-for-a0018eb0* and "Encrypt an Azure Virtual Machine" at *https://azure.microsoft.com/documentation/articles/security-center-disk-encryption*.

If you're not completely comfortable with these technologies but still want to see how Azure Disk Encryption works, you can follow the step-by-step directions in the article "Encrypt an Azure Virtual Machine" at *https://azure.microsoft.com/documentation/articles/security-center-disk-encryption*. You'll be able to encrypt an Azure VM without knowing anything more than what's in the article!

After you encrypt your VMs, you'll see that disk encryption is enabled in the Azure console, as shown in Figure 4-3.

FIGURE 4-3 Disk encryption status, shown as Enabled in the Azure console

You should always encrypt your Azure VMs, regardless of the role that VM performs on your network.

Storage encryption

The previous section explained how you can encrypt Azure VMs. The encryption process for Azure VMs is essential for encrypting specific files. For Azure VMs, those files are the .vhd files that include the operating system and the data disks.

Azure Storage Service Encryption is another option for file encryption. It includes the automatic encryption of all files contained in a particular location, which is similar to whole-volume encryption available with technologies such as BitLocker.

Azure Storage Service Encryption automatically encrypts blob files (binary large objects) when you save them to your Azure storage account. When you save the object to Azure storage, the object is automatically encrypted for you. When you read the file from storage, the file is automatically decrypted for you. You don't need to maintain any keys or secrets—Azure does all that for you in the background. This significantly reduces your security overhead.

Although this might sound similar to volume encryption like you have on a physical hard disk, it's not the same, because encryption is applied on an account rather than on a volume basis. The reason for this is that your storage account isn't confined to a particular hard disk or hard disk array. Your "bits" are distributed throughout the Azure storage fabric and are identified as yours by a customer-specific tag assigned to your storage objects. This allows for greater reliability, in addition to security and isolation of your storage from all other storage objects and accounts within Azure.

The level of encryption used by Azure Storage Service Encryption is similar to what is used in the rest of Azure, which is Advanced Encryption Standard (AES)–256. Encryption is available for all levels of storage redundancy:

- Locally Redundant Storage (LRS)
- Zone Redundant Storage (ZRS)
- Geo-Redundant Storage (GRS)
- Read-Access Geo-Redundant Storage (RA-GRS)

At the time of this writing, the service is limited to a small number of regions, but is expected to be in wide distribution (and perhaps generally available) by the time you read this. Features might change in the interim.

Encryption scenarios supported at this time include encryption of:

- Blob files (block, append, and page blobs).
- VM .vhd files that you bring from your on-premises environment.
- VMs that you create in Azure, such as from the Azure Marketplace or from a customized template you store in Azure.

Customers have asked whether VMs that have been encrypted by using Azure Disk Encryption have significant overhead, because these machines would have double encryption if you also use Azure Storage Service Encryption. This double encryption causes nominal over-head. Although multiple encryption/decryption operations still take place, the overhead isn't comparable to what you see with double encryption of network traffic because with storage encryption, you don't have the protocol overhead also.

The following list provides key facts you should know about Azure Storage Service Encryption:

- Only Azure Resource Manager storage accounts are supported.

- You cannot encrypt classic storage accounts that have been migrated to Azure Resource Manager accounts.

- Azure Storage Service Encryption will not encrypt data that exists in a storage account prior to enabling encryption on the account. If you enable storage encryption on a storage account that already has data in it, you will need to remove the data from the account and then put it back in, because the encryption takes place when the data is actually placed into the storage account.

- VMs created by using images available from the Azure Marketplace are a special situation: the base image will remain unencrypted, but any subsequent writes will be encrypted. Because your private data appears only on the subsequent writes, your information is more secured.

- Other types of Azure storage are not encrypted by using Azure Storage Service Encryption; this excludes table, queue, and file storage options.

In the Azure portal, you can access the Encryption option when you view the details of your storage account, as shown in Figure 4-4.

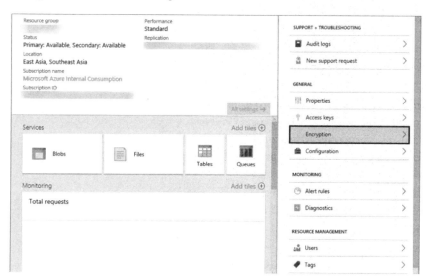

FIGURE 4-4 The Encryption option in the Azure console

Enabling storage encryption is as easy as "turning it on," as shown in Figure 4-5.

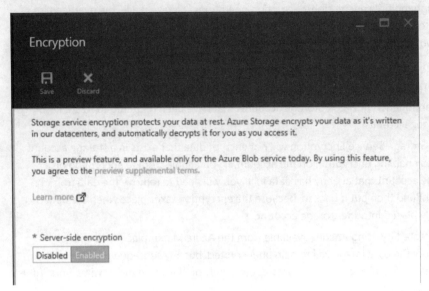

FIGURE 4-5 Azure Storage Service Encryption configuration interface

> **MORE INFO** To learn more about Azure Storage Service Encryption, read the article "Azure Storage Service Encryption for Data at Rest" at *https://azure.microsoft.com/documentation /articles/storage-service-encryption*.

File share wire encryption

File shares have been around since the first file servers were set up in datacenters. A *file share* is a folder on a file server that might contain files or subfolders, and those files and subfolders can be accessed from over the network. The network protocol used to connect to file shares is the server message block (SMB) protocol (sometimes referred to as a Common Internet File System [CIFS] protocol).

File servers are already a challenge to maintain. Often complex clustering and replication is required to support high availability and redundancy. This can end up taking a lot of time, especially when something goes wrong.

That's where a cloud-based solution can be handy. Azure helps you in this area by providing Azure Files. Azure Files use the same SMB protocol currently used on-premises. Server and client applications that use the SMB protocol to access file shares on-premises now can also access information in Azure Files. In fact, you can configure Azure file shares so that they are accessible over the Internet through TCP port 445.

You don't need to set up complex clustering and file replication either, because availability and redundancy are inherited from the Azure storage fabric itself. You can have the same level of replication you have for any other objects in your Azure storage accounts. That's because you create the file shares inside existing or new Azure storage accounts.

One significant difference between on-premises file shares and Azure Files is the level of access control. On-premises, you can apply robust and granular access controls to file shares and you can assign even deeper NTFS permissions to the files inside of those file shares. With Azure Files, access to objects within the share is controlled by a single storage account key that gives the same level of access to all files. There is also no Azure Active Directory support for permissions assignment to data contained within the file shares.

The exception to this is when you want to access Azure Files programmatically. In this case, you can take advantage of the REST API and generate a Share Access Signature for a file share or even individual files. You can do this by creating a shared access policy for the share.

> **MORE INFO** You can learn more about creating a shared access policy by reading the "Generate a shared access signature for a file or file share" section of the article "Develop with File storage," at *https://azure.microsoft.com/documentation/articles/storage-dotnet-how-to-use-files /#generate-a-shared-access-signature-for-a-file-or-file-share*.

Although the access control limitations are certain to improve over time, Azure Files are still useful and highly recommended.

Perhaps more interesting than the access controls you can use with Azure Files is that when you use the SMB 3.x protocol to access Azure Files, you can also take advantage of automatic and transparent encryption of file data over the wire. You might have winced when you read that you could access these shares from over the Internet, but now you know why you can do this safely: it's because all data is encrypted over the wire!

If the client fully supports SMB 3.x, it will be able to transparently work with Azure File Storage to generate per-session encryption keys. The encryption protocol is AES-128 CCM (128-bit Advanced Encryption Standard with CCM mode), which provides some of the highest levels of security available and enables you to confidently access these file shares across any type of network.

Although the idea of using *net use* over the Internet sounds fun, you most likely will still want additional security, if for no other reason than that auditors might be wary of allowing SMB access to private data over the Internet. You can still take advantage of accessing Azure File Shares over the Internet through site-to-site VPN connections. Or, if you want to avoid the Internet entirely, you can access Azure File Shares by using the SMB protocol through ExpressRoute, which was described in Chapter 3, "Azure network security."

Figure 4-6 shows that SMB encryption can be used across any kind of cloud network infrastructure—public, private, or even hybrid clouds.

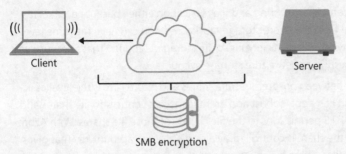

FIGURE 4-6 SMB encryption use across cloud network infrastructures

MORE INFO   To learn more about Azure Files, read the article "Get Started with Azure File Storage on Windows" at *https://azure.microsoft.com/documentation/articles /storage-dotnet-how-to-use-files/#develop-with-file-storage.*

Hybrid data encryption

StorSimple is an on-premises storage solution that can be integrated with Azure storage. You might consider using StorSimple for many reasons, including the following:

- You can use StorSimple as a primary storage solution for your on-premises workloads, such as a file server, collaboration server, database server, and for VMs.
- You can configure policies that offload "cold" data from the on-premises StorSimple appliance into Azure storage.
- You can create automated storage snapshots and have the data backed up to Azure storage.
- You can use StorSimple to help with disaster recovery by installing StorSimple appliances to your new on-premises locations and then retrieving the data you need from Azure storage.

StorSimple is highly recommended as a hybrid storage solution.

MORE INFO   You can learn more about StorSimple at *https://www.microsoft.com/en-us /server-cloud/products/storsimple/features.aspx.*

From a security perspective, StorSimple addresses four different security scenarios:

- User authentication to the Azure storage account where the data is stored
- StorSimple appliance access to the data stored in Azure storage
- Security of the data as it moves over the network
- Security of the data at rest, as it sits on the disk when not being accessed

Figure 4-7 depicts these scenarios.

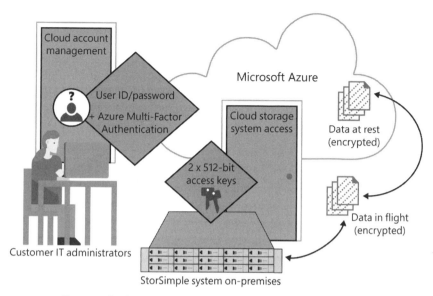

FIGURE 4-7 Key scenarios for StorSimple

Authentication

StorSimple system administrators control the use of cloud storage resources through the online Azure portal. Administrators authenticate to the Azure portal with a user name and password or with Azure Multi-Factor Authentication. Users with access to the Azure portal can change configuration parameters in addition to adding and deleting storage accounts and storage assets.

Authentication of the StorSimple system to an Azure storage account requires configuration of storage access keys. Two 512-bit keys are generated by Azure for each storage account, one of which must match one of the two keys loaded into the cloud configuration of a StorSimple system. Storage access keys can be individually regenerated by using a tool provided in the Azure portal.

By alternating the regeneration of access keys, you can maintain existing connections to Azure storage while generating new keys for subsequent access. For this reason, it is highly recommended that you become familiar with how to change access keys in the Azure portal and in your StorSimple systems. You should also configure Azure to regenerate access keys every 90 days.

It's possible that you have multiple storage accounts in your subscription. StorSimple systems can connect to as many as 64 different storage accounts. You can use multiple storage accounts and their associated storage access keys to compartmentalize access to data in Azure Storage by department, role, team, project, or other categorizations that might work best for you.

Wire security

Over-the-network encryption protects you from situations in which an attacker is able to tap the transmission of data at any point in the network that links the StorSimple system and Azure.

Data transmission between the StorSimple system and cloud storage is encrypted by using Secure Sockets Layer (SSL), supporting up to AES-256 session encryption during data transfers between the StorSimple system and Azure Storage. This encryption is separate from the storage access keys and data-at-rest encryption, although both of these measures are also in force when data is on the wire.

Data at rest

Data-at-rest encryption helps protect you from intruders who gain access to the storage access keys of a storage account and then download your information. It also helps protect you from common situations such as when physical drives or tape media are lost or stolen. With StorSimple, cloud provider employees, contractors, or other entities cannot read data because only you have access to the encryption keys.

StorSimple encrypts data stored in the cloud with an encryption key that you provide, and also uses AES-256 encryption that is derived from a passphrase you define or one that is generated by a key management system for you. Because StorSimple can support up to 64 storage accounts, up to 64 different encryption keys can be used in a single StorSimple system.

StorSimple also performs data deduplication. This can help security by obfuscating data in both the StorSimple system and in Azure Storage. When data is deduplicated in the StorSimple system, it is translated from host-directed storage blocks into content-addressable data objects that are accessed by metadata mapping information. The security advantage conferred here is that the deduplicated data objects are stored independently of the metadata. This means that no storage-level context stored would allow access based on volume, file system, or file names.

When it comes to Azure storage, the data objects in Azure Storage are distributed across many cloud datacenter physical disks. It's not just "pieces of files" that are distributed and easily reassembled. These bits are managed by the fabric management system, and it would require access to the Azure fabric management system to reassemble this data. In general, 16 million objects are distributed across an indeterminate number of cloud storage disks for every 1 terabyte (TB) of data stored in the cloud.

Rights management

Rights management is a mechanism that you can use to help secure the data itself, without any dependencies on the encryption or security mechanism that might be available in the infrastructure that supports that data. For example, you can use rights management to help secure data while that data is in flight, even if it is traveling over a network by using an unencrypted protocol. Similarly, rights managed data that sits on the disk is better protected, even if the disk or the volume itself is unencrypted.

This is the goal of security and where security experts would like to be in the future. This allows data to be easily shared among people who need to see the data, while keeping those who don't need to see the data away from that data. The security is *on the data itself*, and not inherited by another system.

You can get this kind of protection by taking advantage of Azure Rights Management (RMS). Azure RMS uses encryption to help secure the data that you want to secure. Only users who are authorized to unencrypt the file are allowed to do so. This means that data is protected in two ways:

- **Authentication and authorization**   Users must be able to authenticate. If they cannot authenticate, then they are denied access to the data. If they can authenticate but are not authorized, then they cannot access the data. If they can authenticate and they are authorized, then they can receive the keys to decrypt the data.

- **Encryption**   The data is encrypted by using AES-128 or AES-256. This prevents so-called "offline attacks" against the data, which can be used in some cases to circumvent certain authentication-only–based access controls.

Specific files are protected. Files could be text, presentations, graphics, videos, or virtually any other type of file.

User identities are stored in Azure RMS as certificate files. When a user encrypts a document, a small RMS client application creates a content key and encrypts the document with that key. The RMS client application creates a certificate that includes a policy for the document. This policy has the rights for the users or groups and the restrictions on how the document can be used. These policies are template based, so you don't have to create them from nothing.

After that, the RMS client uses the company's key to encrypt the policy and the content key. The RMS client then signs the policy by using the certificate of the user who set rights management on the file.

What happens when a user wants to read a rights-managed protected file? The RMS client starts by requesting access to the Azure RMS service. It sends the document policy and the user's certificate to Azure RMS. The Azure RMS service decrypts and evaluates the policy and creates a list of rights that the user has for the document (assuming that the user has any rights to it; if not, the process stops here).

The Azure RMS service decrypts the AES content key from the decrypted policy and then encrypts it with the user's public RSA key that was obtained when the RMS client made the request to the Azure RMS service to access the document.

This re-encrypted content is embedded into an encrypted use license and the list of user rights and is sent back to the Azure RMS service.

At this point, the RMS client decrypts the use license with its own user private key. This enables the RMS client to decrypt the document so that you can see it on your display.

Figure 4-8 provides a high-level depiction of the process.

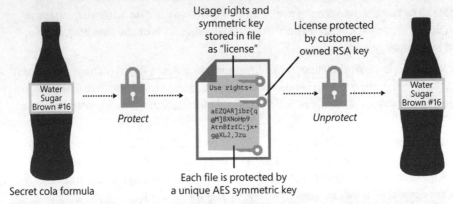

FIGURE 4-8 Encrypting and decrypting data by using Azure Rights Management

You should remember the following four key things about Azure RMS:

- File content is never sent to the Azure RMS service. Microsoft never has access to the actual data.

- Applications enable RMS protection by allowing the configuration and enforcement of access rights.

- Applications use the Azure RMS SDK to communicate with the RMS service and servers.

- Azure RMS takes advantage of Azure Rights Management, Active Directory RMS, Active Directory, and Azure Key Vault.

Figure 4-9 depicts these four key areas.

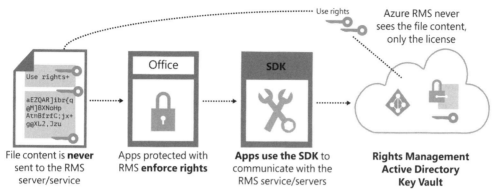

FIGURE 4-9 Four key features to understand in Azure Rights Management

This barely touches upon what Azure Rights Management has to offer, but this book has limited space. It is highly recommended that you employ Azure Rights Management as part of your comprehensive end-to-end security coverage for your Azure solutions that lend themselves to file management.

> **MORE INFO** To learn more about Azure Right Management, read the article "What is Azure Rights Management?" at *https://docs.microsoft.com/rights-management/understand-explore/what-is-azure-rms*.

Database security

Azure SQL Database includes a number of security features and technologies that you can use to enhance data security. These include:

- Azure SQL Firewall
- SQL Always Encrypted
- Row-level security
- Transparent data encryption
- Cell-level encryption
- Dynamic data masking

This section provides a short overview of what each of these features does, and pointers to where you can learn more about each of them.

Azure SQL Firewall

Azure SQL provides a rudimentary firewall that allows simple source IP address access control. This is a popular feature because you can enforce access controls on a network level so that only IP addresses that you deem safe are allowed to connect to the Azure SQL Database server or specific databases contained within the server.

There are two types of firewall access rules you can configure:

- Those that allow IP addresses that you define access to the entire Azure SQL Database server and all the databases contained within it
- Those that allow IP addresses that you define access to specific databases contained within the Azure SQL Database server

The default configuration is to block incoming connections from all IP addresses. You must explicitly configure firewall rules to allow incoming connections from your preferred IP addresses.

The firewall logic is quite simple:

- The firewall first checks to see whether the source IP address in the request matches any server-based rule. If the source IP address is on the list, the connection is allowed.
- If the source IP address is not on the list for the server-based firewall rules, then it checks the source IP address against the list of firewall rules for databases contained within the firewall. If the source IP address matches a rule that allows the connection to a particular database, then the connection is allowed.
- If the source IP address doesn't match any IP address on any of the firewall rules, then the connection attempt is dropped.

You can also configure applications from Azure to connect to your database by using specialized firewall rules.

> **MORE INFO**   To learn more about the Azure SQL Firewall and how to configure it, read the article "Configure Azure SQL Database firewall rules - overview" at *https://azure.microsoft.com /documentation/articles/sql-database-firewall-configure*.

SQL Always Encrypted

SQL Always Encrypted allows sensitive data inside client applications while keeping the encryption keys outside the scope of the database engine. This separates data owners and data managers. Data owners control the data, and data managers can manage the data without having any visibility into it.

Another benefit of SQL Always Encrypted is that it makes encryption transparent to applications. A SQL Always Encrypted driver is installed on the client computer. This driver automatically encrypts and decrypts data within the client application. The driver encrypts the data in protected columns before sending it to the database engine. In addition, it automatically rewrites queries so that the semantics to the application are preserved. This driver also transparently decrypts the data that is stored in encrypted database columns, which is contained in query results.

> **MORE INFO**   To learn more about SQL Always Encrypted, read the article "Always Encrypted (Database Engine)" at *https://msdn.microsoft.com/library/mt163865.aspx*.

Row-level security

SQL row-level security (RLS) makes it possible for you to control access to rows in a database. Access control to rows is based on the user context, such as a user or group. RLS makes it easier to design and code security in your applications.

For example, the feature helps ensure that users access only the rows that are relevant to them, or restricts customer access to only the data relevant to their company. This capability helps you to enforce least privilege throughout your organization and beyond.

Access restriction logic is located in the database tier, in contrast to SQL Always Encrypted, which takes place away from the data at the client tier. The database service applies the access control each time there is an attempt to access the data.

> **MORE INFO**   To learn more about row-level security, read the article "Row-Level Security" at *https://msdn.microsoft.com/library/dn765131.aspx*.

Transparent data encryption

Transparent data encryption encrypts data at rest. As described earlier in this chapter, data-at-rest protection is critical to protect against situations where the physical media might be stolen, which could lead to an attacker restoring the data or attaching a database and browsing the data.

One solution to the problem is to encrypt high-value data in a database and protect the keys that are used to encrypt the data by using a certificate. This prevents anyone without the keys from using the data.

Transparent data encryption performs real-time encryption and decryption of both data and log files. The encryption process uses a database encryption key. The database encryption key is:

- A symmetric key secured by a certificate stored in either the master database or the server.
- An asymmetric key protected by an Extensible Key Management module.

With this feature, you have the ability to comply with your organization's security requirements, in addition to government and industry compliance directives. Transparent data encryption enables software IT pros to encrypt data by using AES-encryption and 3DES-encryption algorithms without requiring the need for developers to change existing applications.

> **MORE INFO** To learn more about SQL transparent data encryption, read the article "Transparent Data Encryption (TDE)" at *https://msdn.microsoft.com/library/bb934049.aspx*.

Cell-level encryption

Cell-level encryption does just what it sounds like: it provides encryption at the cell level. It works similarly to transparent data encryption; however, transparent data encryption and cell-level encryption accomplish two different objectives.

If the amount of data that must be encrypted is small or if the application can be designed to use cell-level encryption *and* if performance is not a concern, cell-level encryption is recommended over transparent data encryption. Otherwise, you should use transparent data encryption for encrypting existing applications.

> **MORE INFO** To learn more about cell-level encryption, read the article "Recommendations for using Cell Level Encryption in Azure SQL Database" at *http://i1.blogs.msdn.com/b/sqlsecurity/archive /2015/05/12/recommendations-for-using-cell-level-encryption-in-azure-sql-database.aspxv*.

Dynamic data masking

Dynamic data masking hides protected data in the result set of a query over designated database fields without changing the actual data contained within the database. You don't need to make any changes to your application to use this feature because the masking rules are applied in the results of the query when they are sent back to the client from the server.

Consider the following scenario: a support professional identifies users by digits used in users' credit card numbers, phone numbers, or other personally identifiable information (PII). However, you don't want all of the PII to be available to the support person.

With dynamic data masking, you can create a masking rule that obfuscates any component of the PII information in the result set of a query. This helps to limit exposure of sensitive data and prevents users who should not have access to the data from viewing it.

However, you should be aware that dynamic data masking is not intended to prevent users from connecting directly to a database and then running queries that might expose sensitive data. Therefore, consider dynamic data masking as a complement to other Microsoft SQL Server security features discussed. It is highly recommended that you use the dynamic data masking feature in SQL Database.

> **MORE INFO**   To learn more about dynamic data masking, read the article "Dynamic Data Masking" at *https://msdn.microsoft.com/library/mt130841.aspx.*

## CHAPTER 5

Virtual machine protection with Antimalware

Regardless of the location of your compute resource, it is important that you use all capabilities available to enhance the overall security of that resource. A defense-in-depth approach is also applicable in cloud computing. For compute resources, this means having an antimalware solution that can help you identify and remove malicious software from these resources.

Microsoft Antimalware for Azure Cloud Services and Virtual Machines is built on the same common antimalware platform as Microsoft Security Essentials, Microsoft Forefront Endpoint Protection, Microsoft System Center Endpoint Protection, Microsoft Intune, and Windows Defender for Windows 10, Windows 8.1, and Windows 8. In this chapter, you learn how Antimalware for Azure Virtual Machines works, how to deploy it, and how to configure it to help protect your virtual machines (VMs).

Understanding the Antimalware solution

Administrators that are planning to implement Antimalware should be aware that they can deploy it in different ways according to the scenario, as shown in Figure 5-1.

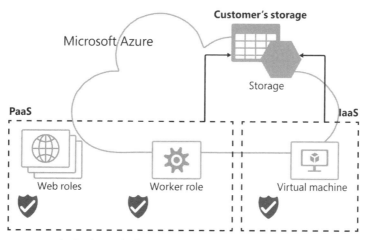

FIGURE 5-1 Antimalware deployment scenarios

As shown in Figure 5-1, regardless of the scenario, the customer's Azure storage is used to store the antimalware event information. The event provider source name is Microsoft Antimalware, which is recorded by the Antimalware service. The Antimalware service also uses the Azure Diagnostics extension to collect these events from the Azure system into tables in the customer's Azure storage account.

> **IMPORTANT** In Windows Server 2016, Microsoft Antimalware is called Windows Defender.

App developers can also use Antimalware Scan Interface (AMSI), which is a generic interface standard that allows applications and services to integrate with any antimalware product present on a machine. AMSI is mostly suitable for in-memory content that never accesses a disk. For anything that actually is located in a disk, you usually need to do a dedicated scan on it only if real-time scanning is off, unless the location is excluded or this file is such an expensive package (for example, .zip or .cab) that the antivirus engine chooses to not extract individual files inside it due to performance reasons.

> **MORE INFO** For more information about the capabilities of AMSI, go to *https://msdn.microsoft.com/library/windows/desktop/dn889588(v=vs.85).aspx.*

Keeping the core scenarios in mind, you can use the following table as a reference to choose the deployment option that fits your organization's requirements.

Azure scenario	Deployment options
Virtual machines (IaaS)	■ Azure portal (Security Extensions) ■ Microsoft Visual Studio virtual machines configuration in Server Explorer ■ PowerShell ■ Antimalware service management APIs (SMAPIs) ■ Azure Security Center
Cloud services (PaaS)	■ PowerShell ■ Antimalware SMAPIs

The deployment options shown in the table are also applicable for daily operations and management tasks. IT administrators can use the Azure portal or PowerShell cmdlets to push the Antimalware extension package file to the Azure system at a predetermined fixed location. One component that runs in the fabric level (Azure guest agent) launches the Antimalware Extension and applies the Antimalware configuration settings supplied as input. This means that you can enable the Antimalware service with either default or custom configuration settings.

After the initial deployment is done and Antimalware is running in the system, the service automatically downloads the latest protection engine and signature definitions from Microsoft.

Antimalware deployment

The first step to deploy Antimalware is to add the extension to your subscription. Complete the
following steps to perform this task:

1. Access the Azure portal and sign in to an Azure account that has administrative privileges.

2. In the Azure portal, select New.

3. In the Search box, enter **Antimalware**, and then select Microsoft Antimalware.

4. Select the Microsoft Antimalware that has VM Extensions in the category column, as
    shown in the last line in Figure 5-2.

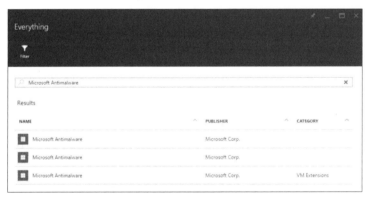

FIGURE 5-2 Selecting the correct version of Antimalware

5. On the Microsoft Antimalware blade, select Create.

6. On the Add Extension blade (see Figure 5-3), you can enter a list of files, folders, file extensions, and processes that should be excluded from the scanning. By default, Real-Time Protection is enabled, and you should keep it that way unless you have business justifications to change it. The other default options are suitable for most cases; you should evaluate how these options match your current antimalware solution on-premises and see whether changes are necessary. After you configure your settings, select OK and close all other blades.

FIGURE 5-3 The Add Extension blade showing the Microsoft Antimalware deployment options

When you provision a new VM and you want to add Microsoft Antimalware during this provisioning process, you use the options that you configured in the previous steps. The same applies for adding the Microsoft Antimalware extension to existing VMs.

Antimalware deployment to an existing VM

For scenarios where you already have VMs running in your Azure infrastructure, you can use the Azure portal to provision Antimalware. It is important to note that VMs created in 2015 or earlier that have an old version of the Virtual Machine guest agent might need to be manually updated to a newer version of the Virtual Machine guest agent before you deploy the antimalware. The older version of the Virtual Machine guest agent has an issue that results in the %temp% folder being filled with log files, and that prevents the antimalware installation from succeeding.

Complete the following steps to deploy Microsoft Antimalware to an existing VM:

1. Access the Azure portal and sign in with an Azure account that has administrative privileges.

2. In the left navigation pane, select Virtual Machines, and then select the VM that you want to deploy Microsoft Antimalware on. A new blade, with the same name as the VM, opens.

3. On the new blade, select Settings (shown in Figure 5-4).

FIGURE 5-4 Options for the new blade

4. On the Settings blade, select Extensions.

5. On the Extensions blade, select Add (+).

6. On the New Resource blade, select Microsoft Antimalware (see Figure 5-5).

FIGURE 5-5 Adding the Microsoft Antimalware extension

7. On the Microsoft Antimalware blade, select Create.

8. On the Install Extension blade, make the appropriate changes according to your business requirements, and then select OK.

   In the upper-right corner, a deployment progress bar appears (see Figure 5-6).

FIGURE 5-6 The deployment progress bar

When this deployment finishes, the Extensions blade changes to show the IaaSAntimalware extension with the status of Provisioning Succeeded (see Figure 5-7).

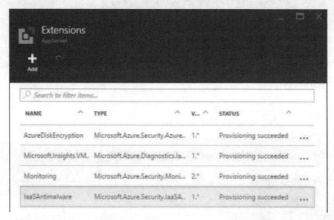

FIGURE 5-7 Extension showing the current provision status

9. To view more details about this extension, select the extension to open the IaaSAntimalware blade (see Figure 5-8).

10. Close all blades and return to the main dashboard.

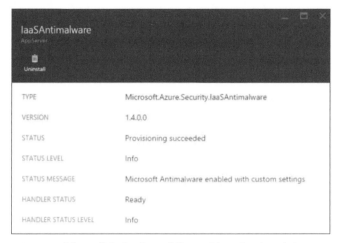

FIGURE 5-8 Microsoft Antimalware fully provisioned and ready to use

After you finish this deployment, you can verify that the provisioning succeeded in the VM itself. You can perform a validation test and verify that the Antimalware process is running in the background. You can view the process by opening Task Manager and going to the Background Processes tab (see Figure 5-9).

Background processes (90)		
◢ ▣ Antimalware Service Executable	0%	1.9 MB
🔍 Microsoft Antimalware Service		

FIGURE 5-9 Microsoft Antimalware Service

By default, the antimalware files are installed in %ProgramFiles%\Microsoft Security Client. The Antimalware user interface (UI) is not available in the VM; however, you can create custom policies to turn the UI on if your organization needs that. You can also use the mpcmdrun command line in the VM itself if you need to perform a manual scan. The following example shows a custom scan (scantype = 3) against an EICAR virus test file.

```
c:\>"\Program Files\Microsoft Security Client"\mpcmdrun -scan -scantype 3 -file c:\
EICAR-131034157784199385.txt
Scan starting...

Scan finished.

Scanning c:\EICAR-131034157784199385.txt found 1 threats.

Cleaning started...

Cleaning finished.
```

Enabling Antimalware through the Azure portal does not enable its diagnostics logs[1]. However, if you use PowerShell for Antimalware to enable it, PowerShell has an option to enable diagnostics logs. The following is an example of how to perform that via PowerShell.

```
PS C:\> Add-AzureAccount
PS C:\> Select-AzureSubscription -SubscriptionName "<your subscription name>"
PS C:\> $StorageContext = New-AzureStorageContext -StorageAccountName "<your storage
   account name>" -StorageAccountKey (Get-AzureStorageKey -StorageAccountName "<your
   storage account name>").Primary
PS C:\> Set-AzureServiceAntimalwareExtension -ServiceName "<your azure cloud service
   name>" -Monitoring ON -StorageContext $StorageContext
```

If you need to deploy Antimalware via PowerShell for Azure Resource Manager VMs, you use the Set-AzureRmVMExtension cmdlet. Be sure to install Azure PowerShell release 1.3.0[2] or later on the computer that you will use to manage your Azure infrastructure. After doing that, complete the following steps:

1. Run the Azure PowerShell cmdlet.

2. Enter **Login-AzureRmAccount**, and then press Enter.

3. If you receive a message asking whether you want to enable data collection, read it, and then enter **Y** (Yes) or **N** (No) according to your organization's policy.

4. When a pop-up window appears asking for your Azure credentials, use an account that has permission from the subscription level. Enter your credentials, and then select Sign In.

5. If this is the first time you are interacting with Azure PowerShell, you might have to run Install-Module AzureRM to install the Azure Resource Manager modules from the PowerShell Gallery, and Install-Module Azure to install the Azure Service Management module from the PowerShell Gallery.

6. If you have multiple subscriptions and want to specify the one you want to use, enter **Get-AzureRmSubscription** to see the subscriptions for your account.

7. To specify the subscription you want to use, enter the following command.

    ```
    Get-AzureRmSubscription -SubscriptionName "yoursubscriptioname" |
       Select-AzureRmSubscription
    ```

8. After doing that, you can use the following sample script.[3]

---

[1] For more information about this behavior, go to *https://blogs.msdn.microsoft.com/azuresecurity/2016/04/19 /enabling-diagnostics-logging-for-azure-antimalware*.

[2] If you don't have Azure PowerShell installed, follow the information in the article at *https://azure.microsoft.com/documentation/articles/powershell-install-configure*.

[3] For more information about this script, go to *https://blogs.msdn.microsoft.com/azuresecurity/2016/02/24 /update-on-microsoft-antimalware-and-azure-resource-manager-arm-vms*.

```
# Script to add Microsoft Antimalware extension to Azure Resource Manager
  (IAAS V2) VM's
# specify location, resource group, and VM for the extension
#$location = "LOCATION HERE" # eg., "Southeast Asia" or "Central US"
#$resourceGroupName = "RESOURCE GROUP NAME HERE"
#$vmName = "VM NAME HERE"
# JSON configuration file can be customized as per MSDN documentation:
  https://msdn.microsoft.com/en-us/library/dn771716.aspx
$settingString = '{ "AntimalwareEnabled": true}';
# retrieve the most recent version number of the extension
$allVersions= (Get-AzureRmVMExtensionImage -Location $location -PublisherName
"Microsoft.Azure.Security" -Type "IaaSAntimalware").Version
$versionString = $allVersions[($allVersions.count)-1].Split(".")[0] + "." +
$allVersions[($allVersions.count)-1].Split(".")[1]
# set the extension using prepared values
Set-AzureRmVMExtension -ResourceGroupName $resourceGroupName -VMName $vmName
-Name "IaaSAntimalware" -Publisher "Microsoft.Azure.Security" -ExtensionType
"IaaSAntimalware" -TypeHandlerVersion $versionString -SettingString $settingString
-Location $location
```

> **MORE INFO**   You can use PowerShell to deploy non-Microsoft antimalware solutions also. Read more about deployment of other antimalware solutions at *https://azure.microsoft.com/blog /deploying-antimalware-solutions-on-azure-virtual-machines*.

Antimalware deployment to a new VM

You can install Antimalware during the provisioning process of a new VM. Complete the following steps to create a new VM and enable Antimalware by using a Resource Manager VM:

1. Access the Azure portal and sign in with an Azure account that has administrative privileges.

2. In the left navigation pane, select Virtual Machines.

3. On the Virtual Machines blade, select Add (+).

4. Select the operating system that you want to deploy; in this case the selection is Windows Server.

5. On the Windows Server blade, select the template that you want to use; in this case the selection is Windows Server 2012 Datacenter.

6. On the Windows Server 2012 Datacenter blade, in the Select A Deployment Model list, ensure that Resource Manager is selected, and then select Create.

7. On the Create Virtual Machine blade, fill in the basic information (step 1) according to your needs, select the size of the VM (step 2), and then in Settings (step 3), select Extensions. The Extensions blade opens, as shown in Figure 5-10.

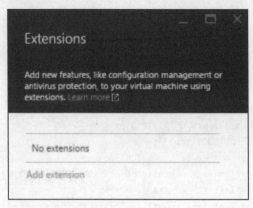

FIGURE 5-10 Extensions blade available during the VM creation

8. Select Add Extension, and then on the New Resource blade (see Figure 5-11), select Microsoft Antimalware.

FIGURE 5-11 Selecting Microsoft Antimalware as an extension

9. On the Microsoft Antimalware blade, select Create.

10. On the Install Extension blade (see Figure 5-12), configure the settings according to your requirements, and then select OK.

FIGURE 5-12 Configuring Microsoft Antimalware deployment settings

11. With Microsoft Antimalware selected, return to the Extensions blade. Select OK to proceed, and then on the Summary blade, select OK again.

The VM provisioning process starts. When it completes, antimalware will be installed on your VM. You can perform the same step by using PowerShell.[4] For Microsoft Antimalware extension selection via PowerShell, use the following sample code.

---

[4] For information about how to use PowerShell to do this step, go to *https://azure.microsoft.com/documentation /articles/virtual-machines-windows-create-powershell.*

```json
{
    "publisher": "Microsoft.Azure.Security",
    "type": "IaaSAntimalware",
    "typeHandlerVersion": "1.2",
    "settings": {
        "AntimalwareEnabled": "true",
        "ExclusionsPaths": "Optional : ExclusionsPaths",
        "ExclusionsExtensions": "Optional : ExclusionsExtensions",
        "ExclusionsProcesses": "Optional : ExclusionsProcesses",
        "RealtimeProtectionEnabled": "Optional : True|False",
        "ScheduledScanSettingsIsEnabled": "Optional : True|False",
        "ScheduledScanSettingsScanType": "Optional : Quick|Full",
        "ScheduledScanSettingsDay": "Optional : Sunday-Saturday",
        "ScheduledScanSettingsTime": "Optional : When to perform the scheduled scan,
          measured in minutes from midnight,0-1440"
    }
}
```

After finishing the deployment process, you can access the VM's settings by going to Audit Logs and verifying that a Write Extensions operation performed successfully, as shown in Figure 5-13.

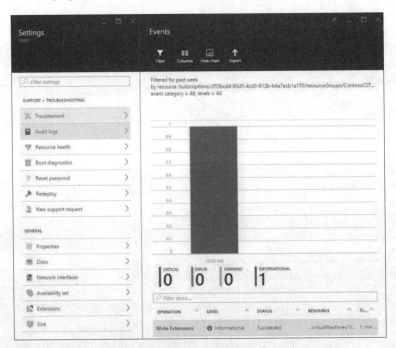

FIGURE 5-13 Write extensions operation successfully performed

When you select the Write Extensions operation, the Microsoft.Compute/virtualMachines /extensions/write blade opens with a detailed log explanation of all IaaSAntimalware extension operations. If you want to view more details, you can select the extension to open the Detail blade, as shown in Figure 5-14. (Some information is hidden to preserve the privacy of the tenant.)

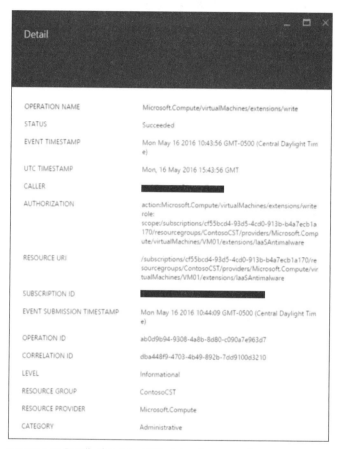

FIGURE 5-14 Details about the Write Extensions operation

This can be useful information for troubleshooting scenarios, for example to obtain more details about the reason the extension failed to install.

> **MORE INFO** The easiest way to monitor your VMs for antimalware compliance is by using Azure Security Center, which is described in more detail in Chapter 7, "Azure resource management security."

Antimalware removal

You can quickly perform the uninstall process for Antimalware by using Azure portal. Open the VM's settings, select Extensions, and then on the Extensions blade, select the IaaSAntimalware extension, as shown in Figure 5-15.

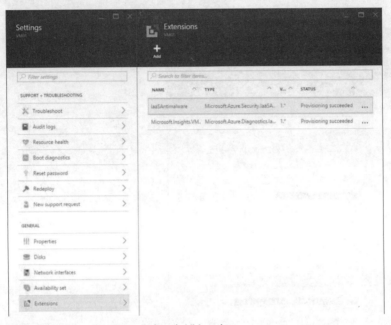

FIGURE 5-15 Removing an extension via VM settings

After you open the IaaSAntimalware blade, shown in Figure 5-16, select Uninstall. When you receive a prompt to confirm that you want to remove this extension, select Yes to proceed.

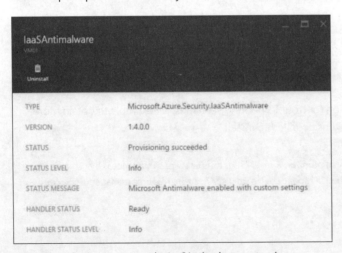

FIGURE 5-16 Option to remove the IaaSAntimalware extension

You can view the Audit Logs again to confirm that the Remove Extension operation performed correctly, as shown in Figure 5-17. You can also use the Remove-AzureVMMicrosoftAntimalware Extension[5] PowerShell cmdlet to remove the antimalware extension from your VM.

FIGURE 5-17 Delete Extensions operation accepted

IMPORTANT As a best practice, you should always install an antimalware solution on a VM.

---

[5] For more information about the Remove-AzureVMMicrosoftAntimalwareExtension cmdlet, go to *https://msdn.microsoft.com/library/dn771720.aspx.*

## CHAPTER 6

Key management in Azure with Key Vault

As explained in Chapter 4, "Data and storage security," data encryption is important regardless of where your data is located. However, when planning to adopt data encryption, you should also plan how to manage the encryption keys because if the keys are compromised, the data is no longer secure. In the cloud, you can take advantage of the Microsoft Azure Key Vault service to safeguard cryptographic keys and other secrets used by cloud apps and services. This chapter explains in more detail how Key Vault works and how to implement it.

Key Vault overview

Organizations migrating to the cloud should keep control of their data's security, and one of the primary elements of data security is encryption. Some organizations also have to be compliant with regulatory requirements for data encryption, for example, organizations that are under Federal Information Processing Standard (FIPS) 140-2 level 2[1]. Some cryptographic models validated by FIPS 140-2[2] are hardware based, which leads some organizations to adopt a hardware security module (HSM). Key Vault might contain a mix of keys and secrets, and access for the two types of objects is independently controlled.

One important concept to keep in mind is the difference between a secret and a key. A *secret* is any sequence of bytes under 10 kilobytes (KB) and used by authorized users and apps to write and read back the secret value. Key Vault stores these secrets by encrypting them with a unique key per vault. A *key* refers to a cryptographic key, such as RSA 2048. The key is used by authorized users and apps to import the key or ask the service to generate one key for them. In this case, authorized users cannot read it back; they must ask the service to decrypt or sign with the key. This provides higher isolation, at the cost of higher latency because every decryption requires a remote call to the service. If your app needs frequent, low-latency access to a key (for example, Secure Sockets Layer [SSL] keys), then the key should be stored as a secret. If your app reads the key at runtime and uses it locally, and the security is more important than performance, it should be stored as a key.

---

[1] For more information about FIPS 140-2, go to *csrc.nist.gov/groups/STM/cmvp/standards.html*.
[2] For a list of validated cryptographic models, go to *csrc.nist.gov/groups/STM/cmvp/documents/140-1 /140val-all.htm*.

As organizations start to evaluate which key management solution they should adopt based on their business requirements and on a solution's usefulness in the cloud and on-premises, common requirements might arise, such as:

- I need to control the lifecycle of my encryption keys.
- I want to control keys for my cloud apps from a single place.
- I need to keep encryption keys in the country/region.
- I need to keep encryption keys on-premises.
- I need to keep encryption keys in dedicated HSMs.

Key Vault is the cloud-based solution for these requirements. Key Vault normalizes the key management process and helps organizations maintain control of keys that access and encrypt their data. In addition, developers can quickly create keys for development and testing apps, and then seamlessly migrate them to production keys. Security administrators can grant (and revoke) permission to keys as needed. Figure 6-1 shows an example of the process.

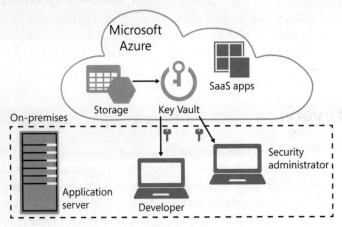

FIGURE 6-1 Key Vault solution for key management

As shown in Figure 6-1, developers can use Key Vault to create and manage keys. This can be done via the REST API, PowerShell, the command-line interface (CLI), or an Azure Resource Manager template. Security administrators are in charge of creating or importing a key or secret, revoking or deleting a key, authorizing users or applications to access the Key Vault, and configuring and monitoring key usage. Security administrators also provide the URIs that developers will use to call from their applications, and provide IT administrators with key usage logging information.

> **MORE INFO** For more information about the Key Vault REST API, go to
> *https://msdn.microsoft.com/library/azure/dn903609.aspx.*

After the developer gets used to using Key Vault to protect the keys and deploy the app into production, scale and quickly deploying other apps becomes easier, as shown in Figure 6-2.

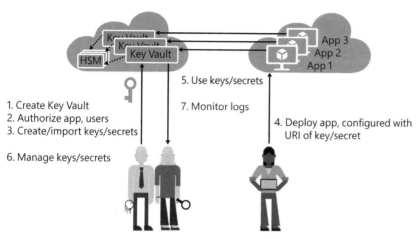

1. Create Key Vault
2. Authorize app, users
3. Create/import keys/secrets

6. Manage keys/secrets

5. Use keys/secrets

7. Monitor logs

4. Deploy app, configured with URI of key/secret

FIGURE 6-2 Final app deployment

Although developers can benefit from Key Vault, other scenarios can also benefit from this key management capability, as shown in the following table.

Scenario	Service
Virtual machine (IaaS)	Azure Disk Encryption
Database	SQL Server SQL Database
Storage	Azure Storage Blobs Tables Queues
Backup	Azure Backup Service

In all these scenarios, Key Vault manages the keys and the secret; however, the customer is responsible for controlling their Key Vault. All requests to Key Vault must be authenticated. Key Vault supports Azure Active Directory access tokens that can be obtained by using OAuth2.

App configuration for Key Vault

As described previously, you can use Key Vault in multiple scenarios, such as the Azure Disk Encryption scenario, which was explained in Chapter 4. Another common scenario is to configure apps to use Key Vault. For that, you need to create a service principal name for the app, create a Key Vault, configure the access control list (ACL), configure your code to use Key Vault, and build and run your app.

Complete the following steps to configure your app to use Key Vault:

1. Access the Azure portal, and then sign in to an Azure account that has administrative privileges.

2. In the Azure portal, select Browse.

3. Select Active Directory.

4. When you are redirected to the old Azure portal, select the directory that will host the application, and then go to the Applications tab.

5. If this is a new app, select Add, and then select Add An Application My Organization Is Developing (see Figure 6-3).

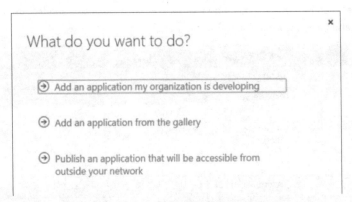

FIGURE 6-3 Selecting the type of application that you want to add

6. In the Tell Us About Your Application dialog box, enter the application name, and then select Web Application And/Or Web App (see Figure 6-4).

FIGURE 6-4 Naming the application and selecting the application's type

7. Select Next (the right arrow) to open the App Properties dialog box. In the dialog box, enter the Sign-On URL for this app and the App ID URI (see Figure 6-5). Then select Complete (the check mark).

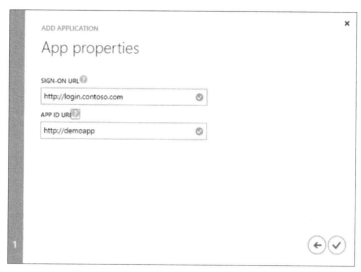

FIGURE 6-5 URL sign-on information and app ID

The app page with the name of your app appears, as shown in Figure 6-6.

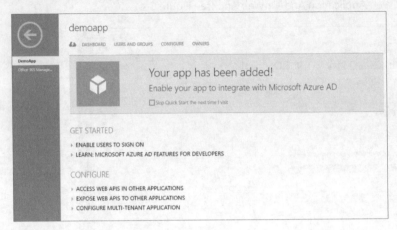

FIGURE 6-6 App page

8. On the Configure tab, near the bottom of the page, select Copy to the right of the Client ID box (see Figure 6-7).

FIGURE 6-7 Available options to configure the app

9. In the list in the Keys section, select 1 Year (see Figure 6-8).

FIGURE 6-8 Creating a key valid for one year

10. Select Save.

11. When the save process completes, notice the value in the Keys section. Select Copy next to this value (see Figure 6-9).

FIGURE 6-9 The key value appears after saving the app's configuration

This completes the creation of the service principal name. Next, you create the Key Vault and configure the ACLs. For this, you need to start Azure PowerShell.

> **IMPORTANT** Always use the latest version of PowerShell from *https://github.com/Azure /azure-powershell/releases*.

Create the Key Vault and configure the ACLs by completing the following steps:

1. Run the Azure PowerShell cmdlet.

2. Enter **Login-AzureRMAccount**, and then press Enter.

3. When a dialog box opens asking for your Azure credentials, be sure you use an account that has permission from the subscription level. Enter your credentials, and then select Sign In.

4. If this is the first time you are interacting with Azure PowerShell, you might need to run Install-Module AzureRM to install the Azure Resource Manager modules and the Azure Service Management module from the PowerShell Gallery.

5. Enter the following command, replacing *DemoApp1* with the name of the resource group that you want to create, and ensure that the location matches your needs.

```
New-AzureRmResourceGroup -Name DemoApp1 -Location "Central US"
```

6. In the output for this command, verify that the ProvisionStage value is Succeeded. Next, enter the following command to create a new Key Vault. Replace *DemoAppContoso* with the name of your Key Vault and ensure that the resource group matches the resource group created in the previous step.

```
New-AzureRmKeyVault -VaultName DemoAppContoso -ResourceGroupName DemoApp1
  -Location "Central US" -Sku Standard
```

The output of this command should look similar to the following (note that some fields are marked with *XXX* to preserve the privacy of the subscription).

```
Vault Name                         : DemoAppContoso
Resource Group Name                : DemoApp1
Location                           : Central US
Resource ID                        : /subscriptions/XXX/resourceGroups/DemoApp1/
                                     providers/Microsoft.KeyVault/vaults/DemoAppContoso
Vault URI                          : https://DemoAppContoso.vault.azure.net
Tenant ID                          : XXX
SKU                                : Standard
Enabled For Deployment?            : False
Enabled For Template Deployment?   : False
Enabled For Disk Encryption?       : False
Access Policies                    :
        Tenant ID                  : XXX
        Object ID                  : 432aed01-79a4-46c7-955d-167f1008f07a
        Application ID             :
        Display Name               : Yuri Diogenes
        Permissions to Keys        : get, create, delete, list, update, import,
                                     backup, restore
        Permissions to Secrets     : all
```

> **IMPORTANT**   Take note of the Key Vault URI; you will need it later.

7. Configure the Access Policy by entering the following command.

```
Set-AzureRmKeyVaultAccessPolicy -VaultName DemoAppContoso -ResourceGroupName
DemoApp1
  -ServicePrincipalName 75842e34-35bf-4e17-80c2-de9d7acb187c
  -PermissionsToKeys all -PermissionsToSecrets all
```

The –ServicePrincipalName parameter in this case is the Client ID that was obtained in step 8 of the previous procedure, when you were configuring the app. This command grants full access to all keys and secrets for this app. This command has no output if it executes correctly.

This completes the Key Vault configuration. Now that you have an app and the Key Vault associated with it, you need to make changes in your code.

> **MORE INFO** If you do not have an application, you can download a sample app for Key Vault from *https://www.microsoft.com/download/details.aspx?id=45343*.

The first step is to open the application configuration file (App.config). Application configuration files contain settings specific to an application. This file contains configuration settings that the common language runtime (CLR) reads (such as assembly binding policy or remoting objects), and settings that the application can read. If you use the sample code mentioned previously, you should see content similar to that shown in Figure 6-10.

```
1    <?xml version="1.0" encoding="utf-8"?>
2    <configuration>
3      <startup>
4        <supportedRuntime version="v4.0" sku=".NETFramework,Version=v4.5" />
5      </startup>
6      <appSettings>
7        <!-- Update these settings for your test environment -->
8        <add key="VaultUrl" value="URL to your Vault" />
9        <add key="AuthClientId" value="Client Id of your Service Principal" />
10       <add key="AuthClientSecret" value="Client Secret of your Service Principal" />
11       <add key="TracingEnabled" value="false" />
12     </appSettings>
13     <runtime>
14       <assemblyBinding xmlns="urn:schemas-microsoft-com:asm.v1">
15         <dependentAssembly>
16           <assemblyIdentity name="Newtonsoft.Json" publicKeyToken="30ad4fe6b2a6aeed" culture="neutral" />
17           <bindingRedirect oldVersion="0.0.0.0-8.0.0.0" newVersion="8.0.0.0" />
18         </dependentAssembly>
19       </assemblyBinding>
20     </runtime>
21   </configuration>
```

FIGURE 6-10 Sample code for the App.config file

You need to replace the following lines with information that was generated during the previous steps.

```
<add key="VaultUrl" value="URL to your Vault" />
<add key="AuthClientId" value="Client Id of your Service Principal" />
<add key="AuthClientSecret" value="Client Secret of your Service Principal" />
```

After finishing it, you can build the solution by using Microsoft Visual Studio and run the application.

> **MORE INFO** For information about Key Vault, read the Developer's Guide at *https://azure.microsoft.com/documentation/articles/key-vault-developers-guide*.

Key Vault event monitoring

When you work with technical security controls, you should ensure that monitoring is also included in the solution. One advantage of using Key Vault is that the events are integrated with the Azure platform; therefore, when you associated your Key Vault with the resource group, events were logged in that particular resource group. Complete the following steps to access these events:

1. Access the Azure portal and sign in to an Azure account that has administrative privileges.

2. In the Azure portal, select Browse, and then enter **resource groups**. Select this option when it appears.

3. Select the resource group that was created previously, select Settings, and then select Audit Logs (see Figure 6-11).

FIGURE 6-11 Accessing the audit logs for the resource group that was created

4. On the Events blade, note the timeline of events and the type of event (see Figure 6-12).

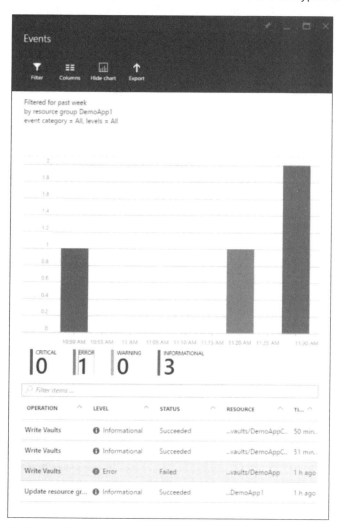

FIGURE 6-12 The Events blade shows a timeline of events and the operation that was done

5. When you select the event (in this case, use the Error event), another blade that has more details about the event opens (see Figure 6-13).

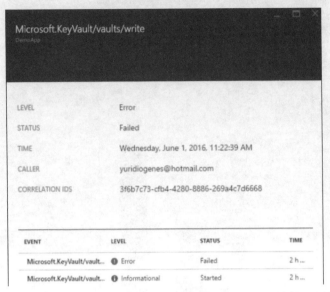

FIGURE 6-13 More details about the operations that generated this event

6. To see a detailed explanation about the error event, open the Detail blade by selecting the event (see Figure 6-14). (Some information has been removed to preserve the subscription privacy.)

On the Detail blade, you can look at the Properties setting to obtain an explanation of the operation that failed. In this case, the explanation is as follows.

```
statusCode:Conflict serviceRequestId:
   statusMessage:{"error":{"code":"VaultAlreadyExists","message":"The name 'DemoApp' is
   already in use."}}
```

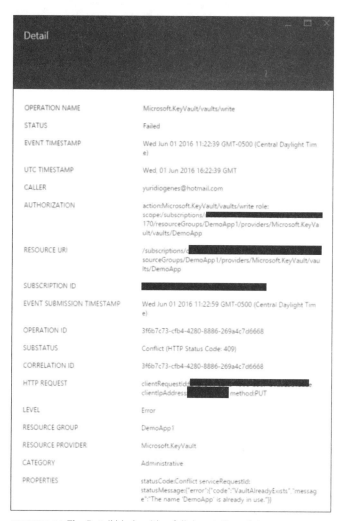

FIGURE 6-14 The Detail blade with a full description of the error

In bold is the explanation for this error, which is a conflict that occurred while creating the Key Vault by using a name that already exists. This error also appears in the PowerShell console immediately after running the command.

## CHAPTER 7

Azure resource management security

Nowadays it is much harder for IT administrators to assess the security of cloud resources, which are often managed by DevOps, distributed across subscriptions, rapidly uploaded and downloaded, and include virtual machines (VMs) and platform as a service (PaaS) services. Because IT administrators lack important security insights, their approach to date has been to slow down or block cloud deployments. Focus has shifted and IT administrators are now looking for ways to help DevOps teams who manage cloud deployments but are not cloud security experts, to ensure that the right protections are in place. In addition, enterprises bring with them the same challenges they have on-premises today.

This chapter explains how Microsoft Azure Security Center can be used for continuous security monitoring and how its integration security management can help IT administrators gain visibility and control of their Azure resources.

Azure Security Center overview

Azure Security Center is an Azure service that can be used to monitor your infrastructure as a service (IaaS) resources, such as Azure Virtual Machines and Azure Virtual Network, in addition to PaaS resources such as Azure SQL Database[1]. Security Center can help you to prevent, detect, and respond to threats with increased visibility and control over the security of your Azure resources. IT administrators can use a dashboard to view the security state of all your Azure resources. This enables them to verify that the appropriate security controls are in place and identify which resources require attention. Figure 7-1 shows a diagram of an architecture overview of the solution.

Security Center can monitor one or more subscriptions while keeping a centralized view of all resources through the dashboard. To detect threats, Azure Security Center uses global threat intelligence from Microsoft products and services, the Microsoft Digital Crimes Unit (DCU), the Microsoft Security Response Center (MSRC), and external feeds. For detection purposes, it also applies advanced analytics, including machine learning and behavioral analysis.

---

[1] When this chapter was written, Azure Security Center was still in Public Preview. New capabilities might be available by the time you read this chapter. For the latest news about this service, visit *https://azure.microsoft.com/services/security-center*.

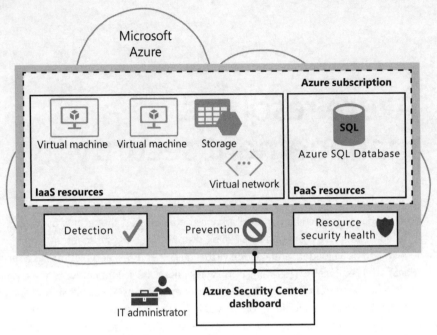

FIGURE 7-1 The Azure Security Center core architecture

IT administrators can define policies for your Azure subscriptions and resource groups based on your organization's security requirements, the types of applications that you use, and the sensitivity of your data. By using these policies, IT administrators can prevent and mitigate threats.

If your organization already has a Security Incident Response Process[2] in place, it can include Security Center as part of its process, because Security Center provides insights into the source of the attack and impacted resources, prioritizes security of incidents or alerts, and suggests remediation steps for the current attack.

> **IMPORTANT** You can use Role-Based Access Control (RBAC) to delegate administrative tasks to other IT personnel based on the need to access information. For more information about this, read "Azure Security Center Planning and Operations Guide" at *https://azure.microsoft.com /documentation/articles/security-center-planning-and-operations-guide*.

Detection capabilities

Security Center uses a combination of advanced detection capabilities that are necessary to identify threats throughout the entire attack.[3] The following table shows the four methods that are used by Security Center to detect threats.

---

[2] For more information about Security Incident Response, read the article "Why Create a Security Incident Response Process" at *https://technet.microsoft.com/library/cc512623.aspx*.

[3] For more information, refer to the paper "A Discussion of Threat Behavior: Attackers & Patterns" by Jonathan A. Espenschied at *http://aka.ms/bupuqk*.

Method	Definition	Examples
Threat intelligence	Uses Microsoft threat intelligence to look for suspicious activity	■ Network traffic going out to compromised networks (such as darknet or botnet) ■ Malicious process executed in the virtual machine
Behavioral analysis	Verifies known patterns and malicious behaviors	■ Abnormal behavior, such as a known process executed from a wrong directory ■ Compromised VM that starts sending spam email
Anomaly detection	Uses statistical profiling to build a historical baseline and will alert on deviations that conform to a potential attack vector	■ Abrupt increase in traffic to a particular service, for example, Remote Desktop Protocol (RDP) connection attempts to a specific VM, which averages five access attempts a day, and increases 100 times more in one day
Fusion	Combines events and alerts to map the attack timeline	■ SQL injection detection via the aggregation Web Application Firewall (WAF) logs and Azure SQL Logs ■ Malicious process identification via crash dump analysis followed by suspicious process execution detection

Management of emerging threats in Security Center

The threat landscape is rapidly evolving, and so is your IT environment. Keeping up with both can be a challenge. The volume and sophistication of attacks continues to increase, and new vectors are being exploited to target cloud resources. Meanwhile, management of cloud workloads is increasingly distributed across the organization, creating complexity for IT security teams tasked with mitigating risk and defending against cyber threats.

Azure Security Center provides the visibility organizations need to assess the security state of their cloud workloads, identifies vulnerabilities and recommends mitigations, and uses advanced analytics to detect active threats. In addition, Security Center integrates with an ecosystem of partners, making it easy for organizations to deploy and monitor a variety of security solutions, like endpoint protection, firewalls, and more. Security information from the organization's Azure virtual machines, Azure services like SQL Database, the Azure network, and integrated partner solutions is analyzed by using Microsoft global threat intelligence and security analytics, including machine learning. When suspicious activity is detected, a security alert is created with details about the source of the attack and recommendations on how to respond.

Security Center researchers and data scientists continuously monitor threat intelligence from across the Azure platform and from customers, and share insights from other Microsoft products and services to identify trends, new attack tactics, and malicious actors. This helps Microsoft keep pace with attackers and innovate quickly in response to emerging threats.

Sarah Fender
Principal Program Manager, Azure Security Center Team

These detections are dynamic and are based on ongoing security research and collaboration among different areas within Microsoft. Microsoft threat intelligence monitoring shares analysis across Microsoft security products and services. Different teams are continuously working in specialized fields, like forensics and web attack detections. The result of this is the culmination of new detection algorithms, which are validated and tuned. This process flow often results in new security insights or threat intelligence that informs security research.

Onboard resources in Azure Security Center

The first step to enable Azure Security Center for your subscription is to opt in by enabling data collection. When you enable data collection in the subscription, all resource groups inherit the same security policy. However, if your organization requires different polices per resource group, you can disable inheritance and configure unique policies.

When you are onboarding new resources, it is recommended that you enable all policies; this ensures that all security recommendations are evaluated. IT administrators are often not fully aware of what is running on VMs in the cloud. When you enable all prevention policies, you receive accurate information regarding the security state of your resources. The prevention policies available are as follows:

- **System updates** This policy verifies whether the operating system running in the VMs monitored by Security Center is fully updated.
- **Baseline rules** This policy verifies the VM settings against a set of security baseline rules to verify whether the VMs are using a recommended configuration. Security Center uses Common Configuration Enumeration[4] (CCE) to assign unique identifiers for configuration rules.
- **Endpoint Protection** This policy verifies whether the VM has an endpoint protection solution installed on it. If it does not, Endpoint Protection suggests installing one.
- **Network Security Group** This policy evaluates your network security group and makes recommendations according to the current configuration.
- **Web Application Firewall** This policy evaluates whether there are web applications exposed to vulnerabilities and suggests the installation of a WAF solution.
- **Next Generation Firewall** This policy verifies the current networking configuration and, based on the current configuration, might suggest an installation of a next-generation firewall solution.
- **SQL Auditing** This policy evaluates your current SQL Azure PaaS solution and verifies whether auditing is enabled in the database. If it is not enabled, SQL Auditing suggests that you enable it.
- **SQL Transparent Data Encryption** This policy evaluates your current SQL Azure PaaS solution and verifies whether the database has transparent data encryption enabled.

---

[4] You can download a Microsoft Excel file with all these rules from *https://gallery.technet.microsoft.com /Azure-Security-Center-a789e335*.

Security Center detection under the hood

Azure Security Center uses a multi-layer approach to detect attacks on your Azure environment. The first layer is Network Analytics, which is used to detect incoming brute-force attacks and compromised machines (bots) that are used for malicious activity (for example, sending spam). This layer heavily uses machine learning to build usage profiles in order to accurately perform the detections. The second layer is Virtual Machines Behavior Analysis, which detects suspicious behavior on the VM by analyzing security events and processes crash dumps. The third layer includes alerts sent from deployed partner solutions and alerts generated by the Azure resources themselves. Lastly, Azure Security Center fuses the alerts from the different layers into incidents, which detail the attack timeline and what the attacker actually performed.

Daniel Alon
Principal Program Manager, Azure Security Center Team

Complete the following steps to enable data collection for your subscription:

1. Access the Azure portal and sign in to your Azure subscription by using an account that has administrative privileges.

2. In the Azure portal sidebar, select Security Center to display the main dashboard (Figure 7-2).

FIGURE 7-2 The Security Center main dashboard

3. Select the Policy tile, and when the Security Policy blade opens, select the subscription that you want to use to enable Azure Security Center. Another Security Policy blade opens, as shown in Figure 7-3.

FIGURE 7-3 The Security Policy blade with data collection options

4. Under Data Collection, select On, and then select Prevention Policy. When the Prevention Policy blade opens, change the recommendation of all policies to On, as shown in Figure 7-4, and then click OK.

FIGURE 7-4 Prevention Policy options

5. On the Security Policy blade, click Save, and then close the next two blades.

Apply recommendations

After you enable prevention policy, you need to wait until Security Center initializes the data collection process on all VMs that belong to the subscription (or resource group) that you selected. The amount of time it takes for this process to finish varies according to the number of VMs and settings available on each machine.

When this process completes, the recommendations are displayed in the Prevention section of the Security Center dashboard. In this section, you can view the recommendations under Resource Security Health or on the Recommendations tile, as shown in Figure 7-5.

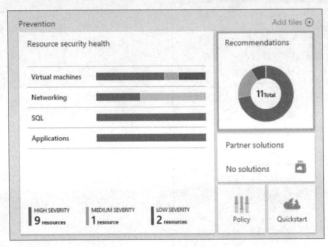

FIGURE 7-5 The Prevention section in Azure Security Center.

To see a comprehensive list of recommendations organized by severity (see Figure 7-6), select the Recommendations tile.

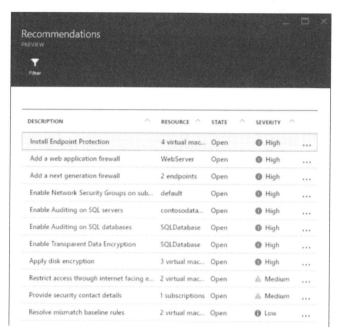

FIGURE 7-6 The Recommendations blade with the entire list of recommendations

The recommendation list gives you a summary of the issue, the affected resources, whether the issue was addressed or is still open, and how critical this issue is. If the recommendations are false positives or are not important for your environment, you can select the ellipsis next to the recommendation and then select Dismiss (see Figure 7-7).

FIGURE 7-7 Dismissing a recommendation

Each recommendation has its own process flow, which means that although the overall experience in viewing the recommendation is the same, the process to address the recommendation might change according to the resource. For example, in place of installing Antimalware in an Azure VM, as described in Chapter 5, "Virtual machine protection with Antimalware," with Security Center, you can follow the Install Endpoint Protection recommendation to deploy an Antimalware solution directly from this dashboard. When you select the Install Endpoint Protection recommendation, the Install Endpoint Protection blade opens, as shown in Figure 7-8.

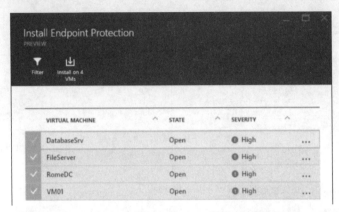

FIGURE 7-8 Virtual machines that are missing endpoint protection

By default, all VMs that are missing protection are selected, and you can deploy the antimalware solution by clicking Install On 4 VMs (the name of the button changes according to the number of VMs). If you do this, the Select Endpoint Protection blade opens and you can choose which solution you want to deploy, as shown in Figure 7-9.

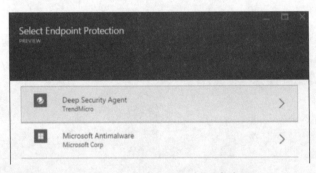

FIGURE 7-9 Selecting an endpoint protection solution

If you select Microsoft Antimalware, the solution will be free. If you select another solution, you must have the appropriate license for the product.

Resource security health

You can also view the recommendations by using the resource security health, which breaks down the resources into four categories: Virtual Machines, Networking, SQL, and Applications. Note that all the categories are displayed only if your current workload has each category. For example, if you don't see SQL under Resource Security Health, it is because you don't have an Azure SQL Server.

The first resource is Virtual Machines, which has a collection of recommendations that are relevant to all VMs monitored by Security Center. When you select this option, the Virtual Machines blade opens, as shown in Figure 7-10.

FIGURE 7-10 The Virtual Machines blade with all relevant recommendations for this type of resource

The Monitoring Recommendations section of this blade shows the status of the data collection initialization in the current VMs. The Virtual Machine section has the same recommendations that you viewed previously in the Recommendations tile. The only difference is the way the information is presented; this view shows the total of VMs affected by each recommendation. The Virtual Machines section provides a comprehensive table that you can use to quickly assess the current security state of the VMs.

The second resource is Networking, which has a collection of recommendations that are relevant to all virtual networks monitored by Security Center. When you select this option, the Networking blade opens, as shown in Figure 7-11.

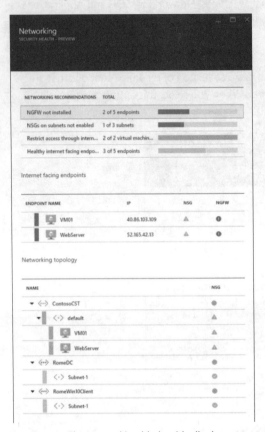

FIGURE 7-11 The Networking blade with all relevant recommendations for this type of resource

The Networking Recommendations section of this blade has the same recommendations that you viewed previously in the Recommendations tile. Critical (red) recommendations always appear at the top. In the example shown in Figure 7-11, the first recommendation is to install a Next Generation Firewall (NGFW). This option uses Microsoft partners that are able to provide this type of solution through Security Center. When you select this recommendation, the Add A Next Generation Firewall blade opens, as shown in Figure 7-12.

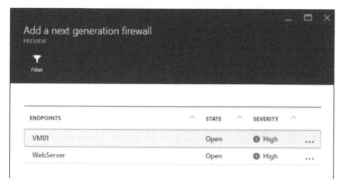

FIGURE 7-12 The Add A Next Generation Firewall blade with the endpoints that need this type of solution

At this point, you can select the endpoint on which you want to install the NFGW. When the Add A Next Generation Firewall blade opens, click Create New and select the partner solution[5] for this recommendation, as shown in Figure 7-13.

FIGURE 7-13 Adding a next generation firewall solution from a Microsoft partner

The Internet Facing Endpoints section in the Networking blade has the endpoint names and their status. From there, you can easily identify whether each endpoint has a Network Security Group (NSG) or an NGFW assigned to it.

The Networking Topology section provides a hierarchical view of the virtual network, subnet, and VM. For each element of this hierarchical tree, you have the NSG status.

> **MORE INFO**   For more information about Network Security Group (NSG), see Chapter 3, "Azure network security."

---

[5] In the example shown in Figure 7-13, the partner solution available is Check Point. You can obtain more information about this solution at *https://www.checkpoint.com/products/vsec-microsoft-azure*.

The third resource is SQL, which has a collection of recommendations that are relevant to all Azure SQL Databases that are monitored by Security Center. When you select this option, the SQL blade opens, as shown in Figure 7-14.

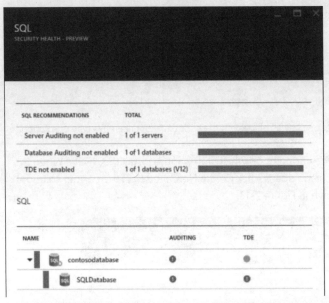

FIGURE 7-14 SQL blade in Security Center

The SQL Recommendations section of this blade has the same recommendations that you viewed previously in the Recommendations tile. The process to apply a recommendation is similar to the resources previously described. For example, in this case, the first recommendation is Server Auditing Not Enabled. If you select this recommendation, the Enable Auditing On SQL Servers blade opens, from where you can identify which SQL Server needs this setting to be enabled. When you select it, the Auditing Settings[6] blade opens, and from there you can enable auditing, as shown in Figure 7-15.

The SQL section of the SQL blade has a hierarchical view of each SQL Server and its database, along with the security recommendations for auditing and TDE.

---

[6] For more information about Azure SQL Server auditing, read the article "Get started with SQL database auditing" at *https://azure.microsoft.com/documentation/articles/sql-database-auditing-get-started*.

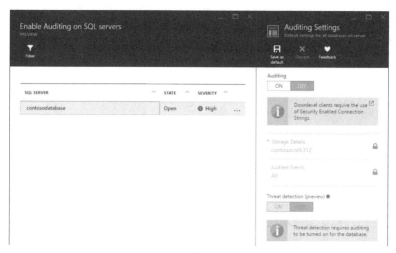

FIGURE 7-15 Steps to enable auditing capability in SQL Server

The fourth resource is Applications, which has a collection of recommendations relevant to all Internet Information Services (IIS) applications running on Azure VMs and monitored by Security Center. When you select this option, the Applications blade opens, as shown in Figure 7-16.

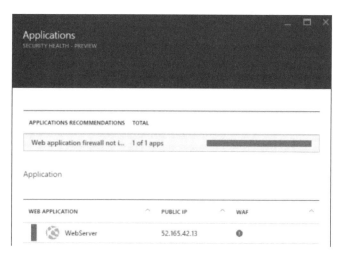

FIGURE 7-16 The Applications blade with the relevant recommendations

The Applications Recommendations section of the Applications blade has the same recommendations that you viewed previously in the Recommendations tile. In this case, the only recommendation is to apply a web application firewall to the web application server. If you select this recommendation, you can add a new web application firewall based on a Microsoft partner solution, as shown in Figure 7-17.

FIGURE 7-17 Adding a web application firewall

Respond to security incidents

After you address all relevant recommendations, your Azure resources will be in a much better security state; however, it does not mean that your resources won't be attacked and that new vulnerabilities will not arise. For this reason, it is imperative to have a continuous monitoring for security incidents in place and use this system to help you rapidly respond to incidents.

> **MORE INFO**   Chapter 10, "Operations and management in the cloud," explores in more detail how to use Security Center as part of your Incident Response strategy.

The detection capabilities explained earlier in this chapter will help you to identify potential threats to your environment. When Security Center identifies a potential threat, it triggers an alert in the Security Alerts tile, which is located in the main dashboard, as shown in Figure 7-18.

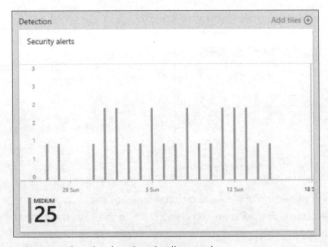

FIGURE 7-18 Security alerts in a timeline graph

The Security Alerts tile shows you the timeline of when the incidents occurred, the severity, and the total number of incidents. This example shows that 25 medium-level severity incidents occurred. To access more information about each alert, select the part of the graph that represents the day you want to view, which opens the Security Alerts blade, as shown in Figure 7-19.

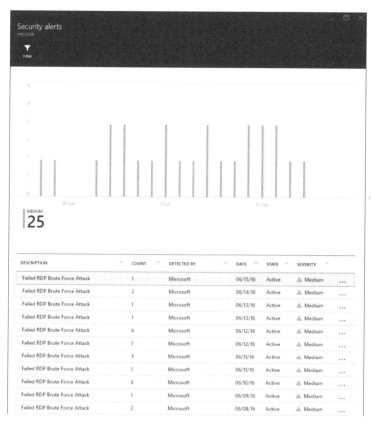

FIGURE 7-19 Security Alerts blade with more details about each alert

Although the alert's graph is the same, the bottom part of this blade has a unique view of the alert with its description, and the number of occurrences for this specific resource on that particular day. It also has the detection source, which in this example is all Microsoft, but it could be a Microsoft partner component. This table also shows the status of this alert, showing that it was not resolved yet, and the alert's criticality.

After you identify which alert you want to address, select it to open a new blade that corresponds to that alert. In this case, the Failed RDP Brute Force Attack blade opens, as shown in Figure 7-20.

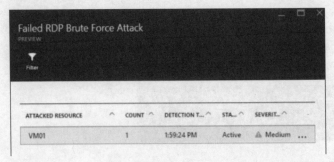

FIGURE 7-20 A security alerts blade with more details about each alert

In this blade, you can see which resource was attacked, the number of occurrences, when the detection was done, the current status of the issue, and the severity. Keep in mind that the status does not mean that the attack is taking place right now; it only means that you did not act on this issue yet. After you do, you can dismiss this alert (as shown previously in Figure 7-7). To obtain more information about this alert, select it to display the complete explanation about this attack, as shown in Figure 7-21.

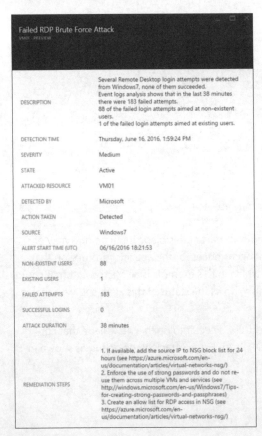

FIGURE 7-21 The security alerts blade expanded to show a full description of the attack

The full description of the attack can help you understand more about the attack, which includes the attack duration, the number of failed attempts, and from where the attack came[7]. You also have a list of remediation steps that you should take to protect the target machine that belongs to your Azure resources.

MORE INFO You can also use Power BI to visualize Security Center data related to your security status, threats, and detections. For more information, read the article "Get insights from Azure Security Center data with Power BI" at *https://azure.microsoft.com/documentation /articles/security-center-powerbi*.

---

[7] In some cases, it is not possible to obtain the information related to the source of the attack. For more information about this, read the article "Missing Source Information in Azure Security Center Alerts" at *https://blogs.msdn.microsoft.com/azuresecurity/2016/03/25/missing-source-information-in-azure-security-center-alerts*.

## CHAPTER 8

Internet of Things security

Previous chapters discussed the general principles of securing assets in a cloud-based environment and delved into the specifics of Microsoft Azure authentication and authorization methods, network isolation and access control, data and virtual machine (VM) security, key management, and security monitoring.

This chapter focuses on an important aspect of the larger environment in which the Azure cloud exists: the rapidly expanding Internet of Things (IoT) that is already having a profound impact on how people live and work. As with any new technological development, IoT has the potential to simplify both personal lives and jobs as IT pros, but it also has the ability to introduce new complications.

One of those complications is how to ensure the security and privacy of the massive amounts of information, some of it very personal, that all of those disparate devices share among one another as they communicate across the IoT. Microsoft is getting ahead of the game by providing guidelines for a strategy that builds security into your IoT infrastructure from the ground up.

Anatomy of the IoT

The Internet, by its very nature, has been an amalgamation of "things" since its very beginning. An *internet* is, after all, a network of networks, and a network is, according to the standard dictionary definition, "a group or system of interconnected people or *things*." What's with all the hype, then, about this new phenomenon labeled IoT? The difference is that up until recently, the vast majority of those "things" that made up the Internet were traditional computers: client and server machines running Windows, Mac, or Linux/UNIX operating systems on desktop or portable hardware.

Over the last decade and a half, smartphones and tablets running mobile operating systems such as the mobile versions of Windows, iOS and Android, have grown more popular, with the BBC reporting last year that smartphones were overtaking laptops as the favorite device for accessing the Internet in parts of the UK. However, these devices are still basically full-fledged computers, albeit in a different format.

The Internet of Things is about connecting a range of devices to our local networks and to the global network of networks. An explosion of task-focused or industry-specific, purpose-built, dedicated devices that look nothing like traditional computers but which contain similar components—microprocessors, memory, and data storage space—are now available, often in miniaturized form.

The IoT will connect personal, business, industrial, and public sector devices to one another and to larger systems in homes and offices where the information the devices collect can be sorted, analyzed, and stored.

Things of the world, unite

Imagine a world where most machines and gadgets are routinely connected to the Internet. Your lights and air conditioning or heating units will be accessible online via your smartphone so you can turn them on and off no matter where you are. Here are just a few of the scenarios that are made possible by a robust Internet of Things:

- You can have a whole system of cameras watching areas inside and outside your home or business offices, and they can be set up to detect when there is motion or out-of-the-ordinary activity, and then send you a text or an email in real time. Baby monitors and hidden "nanny cams" can help you keep watch over your children and child care provider. Businesses can use the same types of systems to observe employees' actions and prevent thefts by both insiders and customers.

- You can remotely set the hot tub to warm up, tell the oven when to start cooking dinner, and start and pause your washer and dryer. You can unlock the front door for your housekeeper, whom you know has arrived at your house because you see her car in the driveway via your IP surveillance camera. You can also remotely tell your DVR to record that special that's coming on tonight, and that you just found out about from an office colleague.

- Consider the convenience of an Internet-connected refrigerator that can detect that you're running low on your favorite perishables and automatically order more, or a printer for your small business that will order more toner or ink before you run out. What about a coffee storage that keeps you stocked with your preferred beans so that you don't have to experience caffeine withdrawal?

- Smart watches such as the Microsoft Band can track your exercise, keep tabs on your heart rate and UV exposure, monitor your sleep quality and duration, and notify you of incoming email, phone calls, texts and social media posts. Your scales can record your weight and share it with your calorie-tracking app on your phone, or even send it to your doctor or share it with your diet support group.

- Implanted medical devices can detect symptoms such as an irregular heart rhythm and report back to healthcare providers or even administer defibrillation to save a life when there is no time for human response. Smart drug pumps can provide insulin or pain medication when it's needed, without the necessity for patients to visit a hospital or doctor's office. IoT-connected robotic arms can be controlled by surgeons in another city or on another continent to perform delicate specialized operations when no surgeons on site have the needed skill sets. The Internet of Medical Things (IoMT) is a whole subset of IoT.

- Internet-connected automobiles can not only collect information about speed, turns, routes, and so forth in motor vehicle accidents, but can also send you email or texts when your oil is low, your tires need air, a critical screw is coming loose, or internal components show signs of wear or impending failure so that you can avoid potentially serious problems. Vehicles can also collect data about weather and road conditions and send that data to social apps to help others select the best routes to prepare for their drives. Businesses can have continuous, real-time insight into where the vehicles in their fleets are deployed, fuel usage, mileage, and so forth. One day, of course, these connected cars are expected to drive themselves, becoming even more sophisticated IoT devices.

- In the manufacturing world, IoT-connected industrial power tools can enable remote fitting, testing, and assembly on factory floors. These tools can communicate with one another to ensure the most precise and accurate adjustment of torque to tighten hundreds of thousands of bolts that must be within specific tolerances for critical components of complex consumer and industrial machines. In these cases, a lack of precision could have life-or-death ramifications (for example, in aircraft manufacture).

- In retail, IoT has already begun to transform the buying and payment experience with point-of-sale systems through which near-field communication (NFC)–enabled smartphones can be used to make purchases. Radio-frequency identification (RFID)–tagged products and sensors can detect where those products are, preventing shoplifting and helping to track inventory and even automatically restock items that are low. Smart screens can detect which items customers are looking at and provide them with additional product information or show them alternative or complementary products.

- Companies of all kinds can not only track their product inventories and their physical corporate assets, but can have that information available in real time to know exactly when deliveries are made or when and where vital pieces of equipment break down and need repair. IoT sensors can also detect workplace hazards so they can be addressed before accidents occur, saving companies money in workers' compensation benefits and possible lawsuits or fines.

- In the public sector, IoT can change the way local governments operate to provide services to their citizens. Smart meters can transmit public utility usage information without the need for a human meter reader to travel around to homes. Smart parking systems can help commuters more quickly find empty spaces in parking lots and garages. Internet-connected dumpsters can let waste management services know when they're full. In law enforcement, IoT-connected dash cams and body cams can help dispatch monitor officers' calls to immediately send help when an officer is in trouble. Sensors or cameras in public places can detect gunshots or other indicators of crime so police can be dispatched to the scene without waiting for a victim or witness to report it. IoT-enabled smoke detectors can send information directly to fire department monitoring stations.

The scenarios represent only a fraction of the many already-existing and potential future use cases for IoT devices. Most areas of our personal and business lives will be touched in some way by the IoT.

Note that some devices or objects, such as RFID tags and barcoded objects, don't directly connect to the Internet but contain embedded digitalized information that can be read by devices that do connect and send that data across the IoT.

As illustrated by Figure 8-1, as the IoT grows, much of what people do and how they do it will revolve around the conveniences and efficiencies that it facilitates.

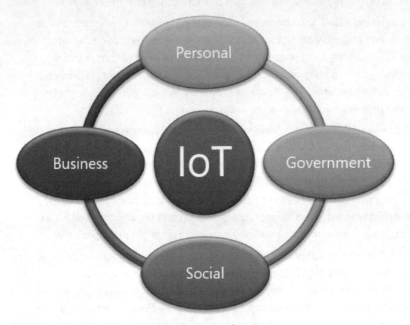

FIGURE 8-1 The Internet of Things at the center of our lives

However, it's likely that in reading through the examples given, at least one or two of them triggered a nagging question in many readers: "What about security?" In fact, almost every one of those sample IoT situations presents inherent security issues. But before you read about the security threats that are specific to IoT and what you can do to mitigate or eliminate them, you should first have a basic grasp of how the IoT works "under the hood." That means understanding the important role played by sensors.

Sensors, sensors everywhere

A *sensor* is an object that gets its name from the fact that it is sensitive to a particular property. That can be temperature, sound, pressure, proximity, moisture, motion, position, light, electrical fields, the presence of particular substances, or other variables. The sensor converts the physical parameter into a measurable electrical signal that can be output digitally.

The typical "thing" on the IoT contains one or more sensors that measure something. These measurements constitute raw data that is then transmitted over the Internet to a location where it is stored in a database or further processed. All of these interoperate, as illustrated by Figure 8-2.

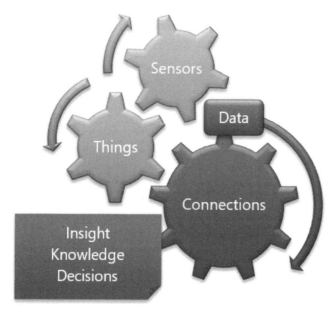

FIGURE 8-2 IoT "things" with sensors that provide data that is communicated across the Internet

Sensors can be classified into different groups, depending on what they measure and how they do it. For example, *biosensors* are based on electrochemical technology. They can convert biological responses into electrical signals and are used in healthcare devices, water and food testing, and other circumstances where measurement of biological substances is required. Another example is *image sensors,* which are based on Complementary Metal-Oxide Semiconductor (CMOS) technology and are used in collecting images and patterns in fingerprint and other biometrics, security surveillance and other cameras, and many consumer electronics.

Sensors are also divided into two broad groups:

- Active sensors that need a power supply in order to operate
- Passive sensors that do not require a power supply

People are surrounded by sensors, although most don't even know the sensors are there. Many sensors are small, some only a thousandth of an inch in size. These are known as micro electro-mechanical systems or MEMS.[1]

---

[1] For more information about MEMS, read the article "MEMS and More: Sensor Technologies that will drive the Internet of Things" at *www.broadcom.com/blog/wireless-technology /mems-and-more-sensor-technologies-that-will-drive-the-internet-of-things.*

Sensors provide the data on which the IoT runs. It's the moisture or flow sensor that detects when you have a plumbing leak and notifies you (or in a more advanced application, signals your device to call the plumber itself). It's the pressure sensor in the hotel mini-fridge that detects that you removed the tiny bottle of water and adds the exorbitant charge for it to your bill. It's the combination of the motion and heart-rate sensors in your fitness band that detect that you've fallen asleep and record that information for you to track in your health app, as shown in Figure 8-3.

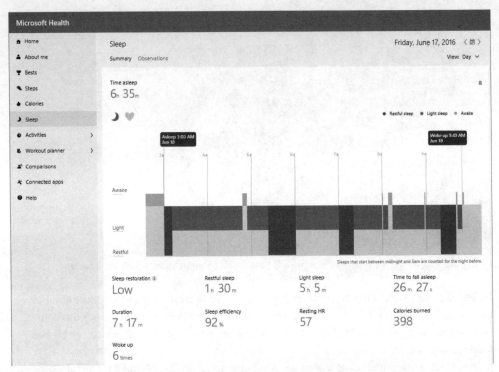

FIGURE 8-3 Sensor-collected data output to applications that turn it into useful information

Some have argued that the IoT should really be called the IoS, or Internet of Sensors, because the real point of having all these machines talk to one another is to get usable data.[2]

Whatever you call it, with predictions that the IoT will grow to more than 38 billion devices by 2020 (up from fewer than 14 billion in 2015)[3], and with many of those devices containing multiple sensors, it becomes obvious that the amount of data that will be generated is beyond the scope of anything that the IT world has handled before. Some of that data will be unimportant, some will be mission-critical, and some will be confidential business and personal information. All of it will travel over the Internet: an inherently non-secure network.

---

[2] For more information about this argument, read the article "Is the IoT Really 'Internet of Sensors'?" at *www.enterprisetech.com/2015/05/08/is-the-iot-really-internet-of-sensors*.

[3] For more information about these predictions, read the article "'Internet of Things' Connected Devices to Almost Triple to Over 38 Billion Units by 2020" at *www.juniperresearch.com/press/press-releases /iot-connected-devices-to-triple-to-38-bn-by-2020*.

Big data just got bigger: TMI

The enormous amount of data that will be collected by the billions of sensors embedded in billions of connected devices means people are at a point of convergence between two of the most important technology developments of the twenty-first century: IoT meets—or more accurately, produces—big data.

According to some statistics, the number of RFID tags alone will reach more than 10 billion by the end of 2016, with projections showing more than 100 billion tags in use by 2020.[4] Cisco predicted in 2014 that by 2018, the IoT would be generating 400 zettabytes (ZB).[5]

> **NOTE** A zettabyte is equal to a million petabytes, a billion terabytes, or a trillion gigabytes. Breaking it down to its smallest component, it is 1,000,000,000,000,000,000,000 bytes (10^{21} bytes).

No matter which way you look at it, that is deserving of the label "big data." And with big data comes big problems—unless you take steps to anticipate and address them. The first problem with data quantities this large is that as the amount of data grows, so does the noise-to-signal ratio. Much of the data that's collected is irrelevant to the mission at hand, but sorting through it all, much less comprehending it, is beyond the capabilities of the human mind and even taxes the resources of our powerful computer hardware and software.

Traditional databases aren't equipped to handle big data, both due to its volume and due to its nature; much of it is unstructured and doesn't fit into the relational database model that served us well for so many years. That's where data analytics comes in. Figure 8-4 illustrates the overlapping relationship of IoT, big data, and data analytics.

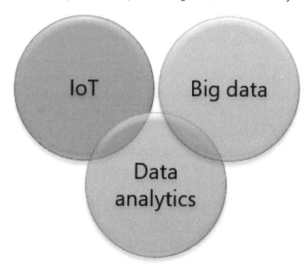

FIGURE 8-4 Relationship of IoT, big data, and data analytics

---

[4] For more information about RFID tags, read the article "The Global Market for RFID 2010 – 2020" at *www.centrenational-rfid.com/docs/applications-rfid/RFID/Markets/Toulouse/IDTechEx/V2/GOOD/ONE.pdf*.
[5] For more information about this prediction, read the article "Internet of Things to generate 400 zettabytes of data by 2018" at *www.v3.co.uk/v3-uk/news/2379626/internet-of-things-to-generate-400-zettabytes-of-data-by-2018*.

Big data analytics involves examining massive amounts of data so that the relevant data can be extracted and analyzed to discover patterns and correlations that will give business decision makers insights to guide them in developing better strategies and making the right choices. The need for effective analytics becomes apparent when you consider the words of Clifford Stoll, author of *The Cuckoo's Egg,* which details his role in the investigation that resulted in the arrest of Markus Hess:

> *Data is not information, information is not knowledge, knowledge is not understanding and understanding is not wisdom.*

Analysis is what turns data into information and sometimes knowledge. Occasionally, it can even inspire a spark of wisdom. Collecting and storing vast amounts of data, like hoarding newspapers and books you never read or shoes you never wear, provides little real benefit. Effective analysis of the data (and pruning of what's not needed) is what makes the data valuable.

Data analytics has been around for a long time, but analyzing big data generated by the IoT is different, due to some of its unique characteristics, represented here by the "six Vs" of big data:

- **Volume**   The sheer amount of data.
- **Value**   Some of the data is of great value to the organization and some is of no value at all.
- **Velocity**   The rate at which new data comes in, making it difficult to ever catch up, much less get ahead of the constant stream.
- **Variety**   Data comes in from many different sources and sensors in different forms: numeric, text, photographic, video, audio, and so forth.
- **Veracity**   Some of the data might be accurate and some might come from questionable sources or be collected under circumstances that decrease its reliability.
- **Vintage**   Some data might be out of date by the time you analyze it, rendering it less relevant.

Despite its challenges, big data has the power to enhance our decision-making ability because the larger a statistical sample, the more accurate the conclusions based on those statistics tend to be. IoT, by providing you with the biggest data of all, has the potential to change the direction of business if you process that data properly.

A comprehensive, high performance big-data analytics solution can also aid you in securing that data, by helping you more effectively classify it as to sensitivity. But analyzing the enormous amounts of data that are currently generated, much less what will be dumped into the systems by the expected rapid growth of the IoT over the next few years, is something that can't be accomplished by humans.

People need machines that can look at data and understand it in a way similar to the way they see it, spot subtle patterns and make connections in the intuitive way the human brain works, and learn from its actions how to do it better the next time.

Artificial intelligence to the rescue

If Cisco's prediction comes true and the IoT generates hundreds of ZB of data, today's already-overworked data analysts might as well give up; there's no way they can possibly keep up. A report from MGI and McKinsey's Business Technology Office predicts a serious shortage of trained personnel with the deep analytical skills needed for this role by the year 2018.[6]

What's the alternative? Luckily, this is exactly the type of task for which artificial intelligence (AI) is well suited. Through machine learning, AI can process and analyze massive amounts of data much more quickly than the fastest team of humans. AI is capable of going beyond the typical software application that reacts in a very specific and limited way that humans have programmed. AI at its best can figure out what to do based on the data it has. Using big data as the basis of its decisions makes it more likely that those decisions will be right.

Many believe AI is absolutely essential to the operation of the IoT as it grows,[7] but AI brings with it its own unique security concerns and challenges that have to be addressed.

IoT security challenges

IoT is big business, and securing the IoT is a big subset of that business. According to a recent Gartner report, by 2020 more than 25 percent of the identified attacks on enterprise resources will in some way involve the IoT. Researchers expect spending on IoT security to reach almost $350 million by the end of 2016, increasing to almost $550 million in 2018.[8]

The security issues related to all the "things" that are coming to populate the Internet are nearly as numerous as those things themselves. Many businesses and individuals who are already using IoT devices have no idea whether they're secure or how to better secure them if they aren't. The lack of security on the IoT is so obvious that it's becoming a subject of popular fiction.[9]

IoT: Insecure by design

To understand the lack of security on the IoT, you should understand how most IoT devices are made. Think about it: smart cars, coffeepots, and microwave ovens aren't manufactured and marketed by software companies; they're sold by automobile manufacturers and home appliance makers. With a few exceptions (such as smart watches), the companies making IoT products have been making the "dumb" versions of those items for decades and understand the workings of motor vehicles or kitchen equipment, but don't really understand the technical details of how the Internet works or the security issues involved in writing software.

---

[6] To read the full report, "Big Data: the next frontier for innovation, competition and productivity," go to *www.mckinsey.com/business-functions/business-technology/our-insights/big-data-the-next-frontier-for-innovation*.

[7] To learn more about this point of view, read the article "IOT Won't Work without Artificial Intelligence," at *www.wired.com/insights/2014/11/iot-wont-work-without-artificial-intelligence*.

[8] To read the full article, "Gartner Says Worldwide IoT Security Spending to Reach $348 million in 2016," go to *www.gartner.com/newsroom/id/3291817*.

[9] An example of this is the book *The Steel Kiss* by Jeffrey Deaver. For a summary of the book, go to *www.jefferydeaver.com/novel/the-steel-kiss*.

The majority of those who create IoT machines speak "security as a second language"—if they're talking about it at all. Because the device vendors aren't tech companies with teams of top coders on staff, and because IoT in its infancy is a highly competitive market and they need to keep the costs of development as low as possible, the software to power these devices is often created in a piecemeal way.

These devices are highly specialized computers made up of hardware, operating systems, and applications like any computer. However, they often run out-of-date operating systems and application software. Worse yet, it can't be updated. That's because in most cases the device vendors don't write the software; they pull in components that already exist and modify them to fit their needs. Much of this code is not actively maintained or supported by the third-party developers who are the original authors.

IoT devices seem simple from the user's perspective, but under the hood, they are anything but simple. That inner complexity is required to achieve the user-friendly outward appearance, because the less the user has to do to operate and maintain it, the more the software is required to do.

Most consumers don't know and don't want to know the technicalities of how their IoT devices operate; they want them to "just work." Even those technically savvy individuals who do want to know often are unable to find out much about the devices' underlying software, because many times it provides no way to access system information such as operating system and software versions, configurations, and update history. There might be no way to force a manual update; you have to depend on the vendor to distribute patches when security vulnerabilities are found. Unlike with popular desktop, laptop, tablet, and phone operating systems, there might be little documentation and no tools publicly available for verifying a device's security status.

Vendors might be secretive about this information for different reasons. In some cases, it's because they really don't know—the support people you're able to contact aren't software developers or security experts and might not understand your questions, much less be able to answer them. In addition, companies might not want to reveal information about the device software because they believe giving that information to the public helps attackers to devise ways to attack their devices. In a more self-serving scenario, device vendors don't want to release information because they know the software on which their devices run is outdated and not secure and they don't want to open themselves up to the possible ramifications of admitting that: customer complaints, loss of business, and legal liability if users suffer losses due to their negligence.

Software composition analysis and disclosure, also called software supply chain analysis, has been suggested as a solution to this problem. Some have even called for government regulation requiring device vendors to publish a list of the components of the software somewhat like the listing of ingredients that food vendors are required to include on the package. This would help individuals and companies that use IoT devices on their networks make a more realistic vulnerability and risk assessment.

Although IoT device vendors bear much of the responsibility for security, users have an obligation to do their part, too. Many users don't think of IoT devices in the same way as their "real" computers, and aren't as diligent in applying updates when they are available. They think these devices aren't security threats if they aren't storing trade secrets or client credit card information on them, but a smart TV connected to the home or company network, for example, can be accessed and used as an avenue to get to other, more security-sensitive systems on the network.

Other problems exist, too. Many IoT devices are severely limited in terms of resources (processing power, memory, storage space). Although this might mean they contain less stored sensitive data that can be accessed by an attacker, it also means they are less capable of using strong encryption to protect the data that they do create, store, and send, because robust encryption requires resources. In addition, the low cost of many IoT devices means they're less well made and more vulnerable to physical tampering.

Most IoT devices today are where PCs were 25 years ago in terms of security. That is, it's not at the top of designers' and developers' minds; they're often more focused on cool features rather than on security, which almost always adds to cost, slows down performance, and causes frustration for users. Unfortunately, failing to make security a priority can have serious consequences.

Ramifications of an insecure IoT

What are some of the potential undesirable outcomes that can result from this mixed method of software assembly and hit-or-miss security maintenance process that affects a significant percentage of the IoT devices on the market? Refer back to the IoT use case scenarios presented earlier and think about the security issues surrounding each of them:

- **Smart home appliances**   These appliances include refrigerators, ovens, washers and dryers, pools and hot tubs, microwaves, and coffeemakers. When connected to a home network, any of these can be attacked and used to provide access to that network and the computers connected to it. Such appliances are also used in company break rooms and could pose bigger threats if used to gain unauthorized access to business networks. Even more worrisome, most of these have heating elements that could overheat and cause a fire.

- **Smart TVs, DVRs, and other entertainment devices**   Modern TVs might have built-in microphones through which an attacker could eavesdrop on the conversations of those in the room, whether in a home living room or in a corporate conference room.

- **Home and office security devices**   These devices include surveillance cameras, baby monitors, alarm systems, and door locks. In addition to being conduits to the rest of the network, these types of devices are critical to home security. If they're accessed, the attacker could shut down your cameras and alarms, open your doors, and gain access to your home and all of the valuables within it. Surveillance cams and baby monitors can be used to see inside your home and spy on what you're doing, listen to your conversations and gather information about your habits, your children, your valuables, and so forth to plan burglaries, kidnappings, blackmail, or other crimes.

- **Home and office safety devices**   These devices include fire and carbon monoxide alarms, leak detectors, and baby monitors. The dangers here are obvious. An attacker could set off false alarms that result in inconvenience or cause evacuation of the premises, giving the attacker time to enter and burglarize the house or business.

- **Smart watches, glasses, scales, and other fitness-focused wearables and home electronics**   Fitness information, including heart rates, UV exposure, weight, and so on is private medical data that could be accessed through compromising these devices. Many of the devices also receive notifications or full or partial contents of email, text, and social media messages that the attacker can read. GPS-enabled devices could reveal the wearer's location. There have even been indications that smart watch motion sensors could be used to expose what you're typing while wearing the device.[10]

- **Implanted medical devices**   An attacker who gained control over an implanted pacemaker, cardioverter defibrillator, or drug dispensing pump could cause serious physical injury or death to the victim. They could administer unneeded electrical shock, dispense an overdose of drugs, or shut down the device so that it fails to perform its normal life-saving or life-sustaining functions.[11]

- **Internet-connected automobiles**   Gaining access into driverless or even driver-assisted IoT-connected vehicles could possibly enable attackers to shut them down and strand passengers or send them speeding out of control, allow them to track the location of the passengers, or divert them to a route of the attacker's choosing. Well-known security researchers Charlie Miller and Chris Valasek gained access into a Jeep Cherokee in 2015, taking control of several of its systems and disabling the accelerator.[12] Earlier that same year, unauthorized access of BMW's ConnectedDrive system exposed 2.2 million vehicles to remote unlocking.[13]

- **IoT-connected industrial power tools and factory robots**   Factory floors are dangerous places where heavy equipment and tools such as saws and compression machines operate. A malicious attacker who took over control of these could cause millions of dollars of damage to machines or cause industrial accidents resulting in injury or death to workers.

---

[10] For more information about this, read the article "Smartwatches vulnerable to hacking says Researchers," at *www.techworm.net/2015/09/smartwatches-vulnerable-to-hacking-says-researchers.html*.

[11] As an example, read the article "Thousands of medical devices are vulnerable to hacking, security researchers say" at *www.pcworld.com/article/2987813/thousands-of-medical-devices-are-vulnerable-to-hacking-security-researchers-say.html*.

[12] Read the full article, "Five Lessons on the 'Security of Things' from the Jeep Cherokee Hack," at *www.forbes.com/sites/johnvillasenor/2015/07/27/five-lessons-on-the-security-of-things-from-the-jeep-cherokee-hack*.

[13] Read the full article, "BMW ConnectedDrive hack sees 2.2 million cars exposed to remote unlocking," at *www.ibtimes.co.uk/bmw-connecteddrive-hack-sees-2-2-million-cars-exposed-remote-unlocking-1486215*.

- **RFID tags**   Passive RFID tags can be read by persons near them who have the appropriate readers, and active RFID chips that transmit their information can be even more easily queried and read, providing attackers with varying types and amounts of information. RFID is currently used in a variety of applications, including credit cards, ATM cards, enhanced drivers' licenses, highway toll tags, and inventory tracking systems. RFID security has improved over the last few years, but some cards and devices still use the older chips.

- **Hazard detection sensors used in retail and industrial environments**   As with home and office fire alarms, attackers could shut down these important safety devices, exposing workers to risks, or they could create false alarms as a diversion.

- **Public sector IoT devices**   These devices include smart utility meters, parking sensors, and dumpsters. Although these devices might not have the potential for life-threatening attacks, unauthorized access to them could be used to inconvenience individuals or prevent them from accomplishing what they need to do (for example, by indicating that no parking spaces are available, which causes them to go elsewhere, and possibly miss an important meeting).

- **Public safety IoT devices**   These devices include traffic signals, police dashboard and body cams, and automatic crime detection sensors. Attacking traffic signals could have deadly consequences if, for example, the lights are set to display as green on both cross streets at an intersection. Attackers could also manipulate the signals to allow their cohorts to evade police, back up traffic to slow down or trap a victim, or create chaos "just for fun." Unauthorized access to the video from police dashboards and body cams could give criminal conspirators information for ambushing officers, and shutting down or setting off crime detection sensors could prevent police from knowing about crimes in progress or send them on wild goose chases to one area while criminals hit another area.

- **Commercial building components such as elevators, escalators, and fire doors**   Elevators could be stopped to trap people inside or sent plunging to the ground at top speed. Fire doors could automatically close to trap victims in a certain part of the building.

This list describes only some of the ways that IoT security flaws could be exploited, with results ranging from annoying to deadly.

IoT threat modeling

Threat modeling refers to the process of setting security objectives based on the value of the assets you want to protect, identifying existing and potential vulnerabilities, assessing the severity and risk of each, prioritizing, and defining and implementing countermeasures that will prevent or mitigate the effects of those threats.

You could think of the IoT as a collection of devices, but there is more to it than that. To perform proper threat modeling, you should consider the entire IoT infrastructure: the full attack surface, as shown in Figure 8-5. This includes the following:

- IoT endpoints (the devices)
- Local networks on which the devices operate (private or public)
- Gateways
- IoT services in the cloud (Internet)
- Applications in the enterprise to which IoT devices send data
- Storage services where the data is stored
- Human operators, including the end users of the devices and operators and administrators of servers and services along the way

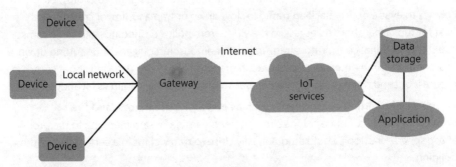

FIGURE 8-5 IoT attacks can occur at any point in the IoT infrastructure

Attacks can target any of these points, not just the device itself. Some of the most effective attacks are against network operations, especially administrative operations. In conducting a threat analysis, it is important to be able to "think like an attacker." You need to be able to recognize what the key targets would be; that is, identify which assets would be of value to an attacker. The next step is to figure out what security protections are in place to protect those assets, and how those protections can be bypassed.

Too many device designers and developers are reluctant to look for vulnerabilities in their own products. To be effective, you have to search for vulnerabilities as if they were prizes. Remember that to the attacker, a vulnerability is an opportunity. Think outside the box; you might have to take a roundabout route to get to the targeted assets.

There are many ways to compromise a device, including tampering with:

- Authentication data
- Application data
- The applications
- The operating system

Of course, one of the easiest and most effective means of gaining unauthorized access is through social engineering. Convincing an authorized user to divulge legitimate credentials doesn't require technical skill, just "people skill." Unfortunately, there are few technological defenses; preventing socially engineered attacks hinges on educating users.

After you identify a vulnerability, it's time to shift your mindset and "think like a protector." During the vulnerability detection phase, you were playing offense; now you're playing on the defensive team. Don't ignore the obvious, such as physical security. IoT devices, because of their widespread physical distribution, are particularly vulnerable to physical breach. An attacker can steal one, reverse-engineer it, and use the information to attack other devices of the same type.

As identity is the key to authenticating people, it's also key to securing IoT devices. It is important that devices have unique assigned identifying information that can't be changed or spoofed to prevent the use of the same security credentials across numbers of devices of the same type. This should be a given, but given the immaturity of the IoT and the lack of focus on security by many of its vendors, that's not the case.

Elements of a secure IoT infrastructure include management of device identities and their associated credentials, policies, a device platform that supports security mechanisms, an operating system designed with security in mind, robust hardware, and a development framework that incorporates security from the ground up.

Windows 10 IoT and Azure IoT

The commitment of Microsoft to the Internet of Things is evident in its current offering of IoT-focused products and services. The investment in security is evident in its longstanding Trustworthy Computing initiative, established by Bill Gates in 2002.[14] This has evolved into the SD3 security development lifecycle principles (secure by design, secure by default, secure in deployment), and culminated in the Microsoft Cybersecurity Commitment, published in January 2015. In this commitment, the company outlines its security and privacy fundamentals regarding

---

[14] To read the full initiative, "TwC Next: Marking a Milestone. Continuing our Commitment," go to *https://www.microsoft.com/en-us/twc/twcnext/default.aspx*.

software development, cloud operations, malware protection, security response, product and cloud security, and security expertise.[15]

Microsoft brings almost a decade and a half of trustworthy computing to its reimagined vision as a "cloud first, mobile first" devices and services company. That experience and dedication to security form the foundation for Windows 10 IoT and Azure IoT Suite.

Windows 10 IoT editions

Windows 10 IoT is, according to Microsoft documentation, "a family of Windows 10 editions targeted towards a wide range of intelligent devices, from small industrial gateways to larger more complex devices like point of sales terminals and ATMs." These consist of three iterations:

- Windows 10 IoT Enterprise
- Windows 10 IoT Mobile Enterprise
- Windows 10 IoT Core

Windows 10 was designed to work with all types of devices as part of the "One Windows" philosophy that brings the same universal apps to both traditional desktop and mobile devices and IoT dedicated devices, along with IoT gateways. Windows 10 connectivity is supported for device-to-device, device-to-cloud, and sensor-to-device communications, and is built on open device interoperability standards.

The Windows 10 IoT Enterprise edition supports classic Windows applications, in addition to universal apps, and runs a variety of industry devices. Windows 10 IoT Mobile Enterprise edition is created for line-of-business mobile devices and supports barcode scanners and other peripherals for retail, healthcare, manufacturing, and other industry-specific applications. Windows 10 IoT Core is designed as a more minimalist operating system for small, low-cost devices that run a single line-of-business application.

---

[15] To learn more about this commitment, read the article "MSDN TV: Thinking About Security - Secure by Design, Secure by Default, Secure in Deployment and Communications" at *https://www.microsoft.com/en-us/download/details.aspx?id=21629*.

Windows IoT Core provides identity and access controls through Windows Hello and Microsoft Passport, with the added security of multifactor authentication. It also supports Credential Guard to protect users' credentials via virtualization-based security (VBS). IoT data is protected by BitLocker and BitLocker to Go, in addition to file-level encryption and Rights Management Services (RMS). Of course, data in transit is protected by IPsec and VPNs. Further, new and enhanced features in Windows 10, such as Device Guard, VBS, and the Microsoft Edge browser, along with Windows Defender, protect the system from malware.

Windows 10 was designed to be the most secure operating system from Microsoft, with enterprise grade security built in under the guidance of end-to-end security expert engagement. Some of the defenses enhanced or introduced in Windows 10 include Secure Boot, BitLocker, Device Guard, and Credential Guard, in addition to the ability to lock down access to unauthorized peripherals.

The Windows 10 IoT editions are designed to work with Azure IoT services.

Azure IoT Suite and secure Azure IoT infrastructure

The Azure IoT Suite is a set of tools with which you can monitor your IoT devices, capture and analyze the information, and then use the information to discover patterns and correlations that provide better insight into your business processes.

The Azure IoT Suite is built on the Azure cloud infrastructure, which in turn is built upon the Security Development Lifecycle (SDL), and operates in conjunction with the Microsoft Operational Security Assurance process and Cyber Defense Operations Center, putting device security and cloud security at the forefront of Azure IoT technology engineering.

Azure provides machine learning, data analytics, data storage, and networking—the components that are necessary to a more secure IoT infrastructure—protected by the Microsoft software security "red team" that is constantly testing to uncover emerging threats and vulnerabilities, and the global incident response team that takes action to mitigate effects of attacks.

Some of the security mechanisms in Azure include:

- Continual intrusion detection and prevention
- Service attack prevention
- Penetration testing
- Forensics tools
- Multi-Factor Authentication

Azure IoT Suite builds on the inherent security focus in Azure to secure your IoT deployments at the device level, at the connection level, and at the cloud level, as shown in more detail in Table 8-1.[16]

TABLE 8-1 Azure IoT Security

Device security	Connection security	Cloud security
Unique identity key for each device	Industry-standard encryption technologies	Azure Active Directory (Azure AD)
Azure IoT Hub Registry	TLS/X.509 certificates	Policy-based authorization model
Secure storage of device identities and security keys	Acknowledgments in response to messages	Flexible management of security keys
Access control policies in the cloud	Message caching (7 days for telemetry, 2 for commands)	Easy, auditable, reviewable access management
Activation and deactivation of device identities	Industry standard HTTPS and Advanced Message Queuing Protocol	More secure cloud storage of security keys
Devices do not accept unsolicited connections	More secure connection to both IP-enabled and non-IP-enabled devices	Data stored in database formats that enable defining security levels
Devices connect to well-known services only	Durability of messaging	Monitoring and auditing of intrusions or access to data

NOTE Non-IP-enabled devices connect over Bluetooth or other short-range protocols.

The Azure IoT Suite secure device provisioning gets your IoT implementation off to a more secure start by generating a key that is associated with the unique device ID. There are two types of device IDs: physical and logical. The physical ID can be flashed into the memory of a hardware trust module so that it will be difficult to change. You can also establish logical device IDs.

---

[16] For more information about IoT security in Azure, read the blog post "How Microsoft Azure engineers for IoT security" at *https://blogs.microsoft.com/iot/2016/03/24/how-microsoft-azure-engineers-for-iot-security*.

The identities and their corresponding keys are stored in the Azure IoT Hub identity registry. Here, you can manage the identities and control their access by adding them to allow or block lists. The Hub policies also enable you to disable individual device identities. You can revoke access credentials and permissions almost instantaneously.

For better security, devices establish connections as outbound-only. Commands cannot be received by a device unless it explicitly establishes a connection, and then when the connection is established, communications can take place in both directions. The Hub doesn't initiate communications with the devices; instead, it waits for the device to connect to receive commands. The command can be stored for up to two days.

The Internet of Things and the myriad of devices connected to it are changing the way people communicate, gather information, and make personal and business decisions. IoT devices come in an endless number of forms, from full-fledged computers running desktop operating systems to tiny single-purpose devices running stripped-down operating systems. Securing the IoT is complicated by the diversity of hardware and software, in addition to the lack of focus on security demonstrated by some manufacturers of IoT devices.

Responsibility for the security of the IoT infrastructure is, by necessity, a shared one. The IoT hardware manufacturers or integrators; the IoT developers and deployment specialists; the IoT operators who run, monitor, update, maintain and troubleshoot the IoT solution; in addition to the cloud provider, local network administrators, and end-users of the devices must all do their part to follow security best practices to thwart attackers who target all points within the IoT infrastructure.

Windows 10 IoT editions and Azure IoT Suite running on Microsoft Azure include security features and tools that can help businesses deploy IoT more securely. This chapter provides a high-level overview of how the IoT works, the security issues and challenges inherent in the sudden influx of "things" onto the Internet, threat modeling for IoT, and how Microsoft IoT-related products and services can help to protect the ever-expanding number of "things" on the Internet.

## CHAPTER 9

Hybrid environment monitoring

So far, the capabilities covered in this book relate to resources running in the Microsoft Azure platform. However, many companies need to use Microsoft threat intelligence and security monitoring capabilities to monitor on-premises resources or resources running in a different cloud solution, such as Amazon Web Services (AWS). For these scenarios, you can use Operations Management Suite (OMS) Security and Audit solution.

This chapter explains how OMS Security and Audit solution can be used for continuous security monitoring in a hybrid environment and how it can assist IT administrators in gaining visibility and control of their resources.

Operations Management Suite Security and Audit solution overview

OMS Security and Audit solution collects security-related data from virtually any source, regardless of volume, format, or location. After collecting the data, OMS analyzes it and provides a dashboard for data visualization. By using Microsoft threat intelligence, OMS provides insights that can help you determine whether you have a compromised resource in your environment, as shown in Figure 9-1.

The following list summarizes what you need to get started with the OMS Security and Audit solution:

- An Azure subscription to use Log Analytics[1]
- An OMS workspace, which is a logical container where your management data is stored
- A connection from your Windows or Linux computers to your OMS workspace
- A user OMS Security and Audit solution to monitor your resources

---

[1] For more information about Log Analytics, read the article "Get started with Log Analytics" at *https://azure.microsoft.com/documentation/articles/log-analytics-get-started*.

Chapter 7, "Azure resource management security," described Azure Security Center, which provides security management, including policies, security assessment, and threat detection, for Azure resources. Security Center is built in to Azure, and basic monitoring is available at no charge. OMS offers security insights and threat detection across on-premises and cloud IT environments, including private and public datacenters. Based on their needs, customers could choose to use one or both solutions.

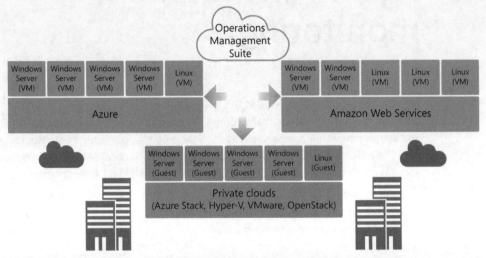

FIGURE 9-1 Typical scenario where OMS is the most appropriate solution

At the time this chapter was written, these two solutions were separated; over time, the same capabilities will be available in both OMS and Azure, providing a single security management and monitoring solution that can be used to protect the customers' entire IT environment, including workloads running in private and public datacenters (Azure and AWS).

Log Analytics configuration

Log Analytics is a service in OMS that helps you to collect and analyze data generated by resources in the cloud and on-premises environments. To use Log Analytics, you need a paid Azure subscription. Complete the following steps to configure Log Analytics:

1. Access the Azure portal and sign in to the subscription account that has administrative privileges.

2. In the Azure portal, select Browse.

3. Enter **Log**, and when Log Analytics (OMS) appears, select it. The Log Analytics (OMS) blade opens, as shown in Figure 9-2.

FIGURE 9-2 The Log Analytics blade

4. Select Add. The OMS Workspace blade opens, as shown in Figure 9-3.

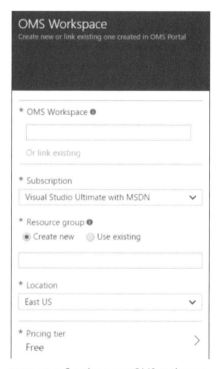

FIGURE 9-3 Creating a new OMS workspace

5. In the OMS Workspace text box, enter a unique name for this workspace (or link to an existing one if you already have it), and then select the subscription and the resource group that you want to use for this workspace or select an existing one.

6. Select the location in which you want to store the workspace and the pricing tier. When you finish setting all the options, select Create to display the details of the workspace, as shown in Figure 9-4.

FIGURE 9-4 OMS workspace details, with the subscription and workspace information masked for privacy purposes

At this point, you finished the first configuration step for OMS. Now you have an OMS workspace to store your data. The second step is to configure the computers that will be monitored by OMS, which is described in the next section.

Windows Agent installation

Although you can monitor Windows and Linux systems in OMS,[2] this book describes the steps to install the agent only on a Windows system. The following steps guide you through the addition of OMS Solutions,[3] which include the Security and Audit solution and the installation of the Windows agent:

1. In the OMS Workspace blade, select OMS Portal. A new browser tab (or window, depending on your browser configuration) opens.

---

[2] For more information about the Linux agent, read the article "Connect Linux computers to Log Analytics" at *https://azure.microsoft.com/documentation/articles/log-analytics-linux-agents*.

[3] For more information about OMS Solutions. read the article "Add Log Analytics solutions from the Solutions Gallery" at *https://azure.microsoft.com/documentation/articles/log-analytics-add-solutions*.

2. If prompted, sign in by using your Azure subscription credentials. The window opens to the Microsoft Operations Management Suite dashboard, as shown in Figure 9-5.

FIGURE 9-5 The OMS main dashboard

3. On the left side of the dashboard, select Solutions Gallery. Ensure that the solutions shown in Figure 9-6 are added (showing as *owned*). If you don't see a solution here, click **Visit the Gallery** at the bottom of this list to add it.

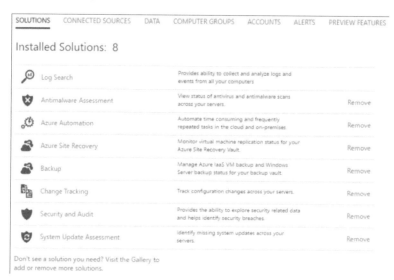

FIGURE 9-6 OMS solutions

4. Select Home (the house icon in the left navigation pane), and then select Settings.

5. On the Connected Sources tab, shown in Figure 9-7, download the appropriate Windows agent (64-bit or 32-bit). Copy the Workspace ID and the Primary Key by clicking the Copy button, and then paste them in a Notepad file. These values are used later during the agent installation.

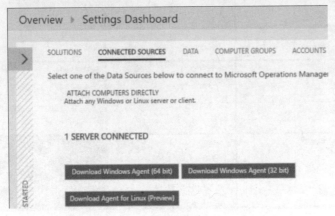

FIGURE 9-7 Selecting the appropriate Windows agent

6. For this example, you will be using the Windows Agent 64-bit (MMASetup-AMD64.exe file) and installing it in a Windows Server 2012 computer. After manually copying this file to the destination system, double-click it and then select Next on the Welcome To The Microsoft Monitoring Agent Setup Wizard page.

7. Read the license and terms, and then select I Agree.

8. On the Destination Folder page, select the destination folder or leave the default selection, and click Next.

9. On the Agent Setup Options page, select the Connect The Agent To Microsoft Azure Operational Insights check box, and click Next.

10. On the Azure Operational Insights page, shown in Figure 9-8, enter the workspace ID (saved in step 5). In the Workspace Key box, enter the primary key (also saved in step 5), and then click Next.

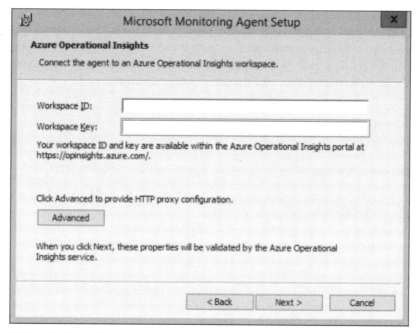

FIGURE 9-8 Connecting the agent to the OMS workspace ID

> **IMPORTANT** If this computer is behind a proxy, be sure to select Advanced and enter Specify The Proxy Configuration.

11. On the Ready To Install page, select Install.

12. When the Microsoft Monitoring Agent Configuration Completed Successfully page appears, select Finish.

> **MORE INFO** You can also deploy the agent by using a command-line interface (CLI) or PowerShell. For more information about automating this process, read the article "Connect Windows computers to Log Analytics" at *https://azure.microsoft.com/documentation/articles/log-analytics-windows-agents*.

Resource monitoring using OMS Security and Audit solution

After you configure your environment so that all computers report to OMS, you can use the Security and Audit solution to closely monitor your resources. Open the OMS Portal (step 1 in the previous section). On the main dashboard are tiles that represent solutions; for example, the Malware Assessment tile includes items managed by the Malware Assessment solution. The number of dashboard tiles varies according to the number of solutions you have.

In a hybrid environment where you want to more securely manage resources that are on-premises and in the cloud, you use the Security and Audit solution. The information available in the tile varies according to the environment. Figure 9-9 shows an example of 16 computers active in the last 24 hours and an increase of 198 in the number of accounts authenticated in the last 24 hours. To access this solution, click the Security And Audit tile.

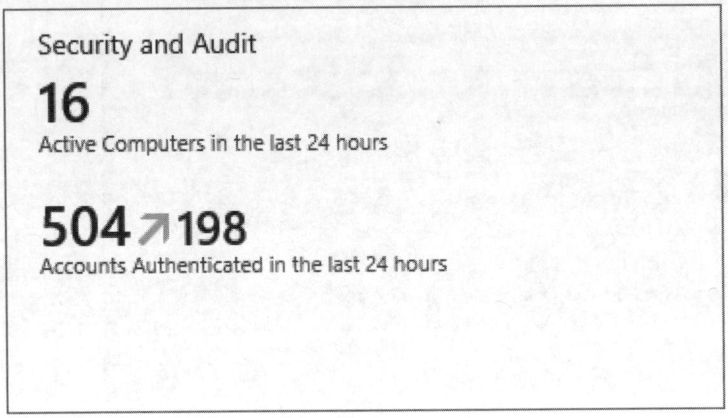

Security and Audit

16

Active Computers in the last 24 hours

504 ↗ 198

Accounts Authenticated in the last 24 hours

FIGURE 9-9 Accessing an OMS Security and Audit solution

The solution dashboard is divided into four sections:

- **Security Domains**   This section provides an overview of security records over time, antimalware assessment, update assessment, identity and access information, computers with security events, and access to Azure Security Center.
- **Notable Issues**   This section provides a security alert overview ranked by criticality.
- **Threat Intelligence**   This section provides an instant threat map that uses the Microsoft threat intelligence capability to provide information regarding potential threats in your environment.
- **Common Security Threats**   This section includes a predefined list of queries that can assist you in finding security-related activities in your environment.

Security state monitoring

One of the biggest challenges to monitor resources located in multiple locations (cloud and on-premises) is to aggregate all resources in a single console and easily find the security state of these resources. The security state of a computer can include identification of the current state of the antimalware solution in the target computers, the system's updates, and security-related events.

To access the antimalware state of the computers, select the Antimalware Assessment tile. A dashboard similar to the one shown in Figure 9-10 is displayed.

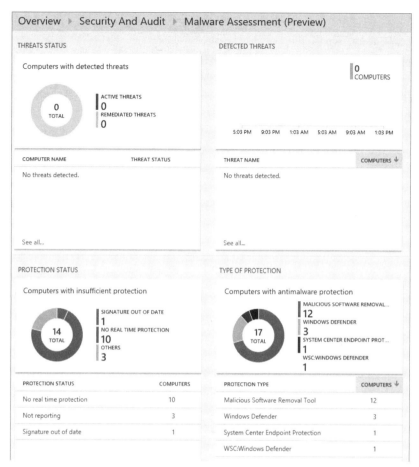

Overview ▶ Security And Audit ▶ Malware Assessment (Preview)

THREATS STATUS

Computers with detected threats

0
TOTAL

ACTIVE THREATS
0
REMEDIATED THREATS
0

COMPUTER NAME	THREAT STATUS
No threats detected.	

See all...

DETECTED THREATS

0
COMPUTERS

5:03 PM   9:03 PM   1:03 AM   5:03 AM   9:03 AM   1:03 PM

THREAT NAME	COMPUTERS ↓
No threats detected.	

See all...

PROTECTION STATUS

Computers with insufficient protection

14
TOTAL

SIGNATURE OUT OF DATE
1
NO REAL TIME PROTECTION
10
OTHERS
3

PROTECTION STATUS	COMPUTERS
No real time protection	10
Not reporting	3
Signature out of date	1

TYPE OF PROTECTION

Computers with antimalware protection

17
TOTAL

MALICIOUS SOFTWARE REMOVAL...
12
WINDOWS DEFENDER
3
SYSTEM CENTER ENDPOINT PROT...
1
WSC:WINDOWS DEFENDER
1

PROTECTION TYPE	COMPUTERS ↓
Malicious Software Removal Tool	12
Windows Defender	3
System Center Endpoint Protection	1
WSC:Windows Defender	1

FIGURE 9-10 The Malware Assessment dashboard

This dashboard gives you a comprehensive view of major elements related to antimalware assessment. From the Threats Status tile, you can easily identify active threats (red) in your environment and remediated threats (yellow). The Detected Threats tile has a list of all threats detected and which computers were compromised by those threats. From the Protection Status tile, you can identify computers that have out of date antimalware signatures and computers without any antimalware protection. The Type Of Protection tile shows what type of endpoint protection is used by each monitored computer. With this information available in a single dashboard, you can easily assess your environment. If you need to investigate further, you can select each tile for more details.

However, having a system with antimalware installed is usually not enough. Many threats try to exploit known vulnerabilities, such as attacking an unpatched system. To access the current state of your systems, select the Update Assessment tile to display a dashboard similar to Figure 9-11.

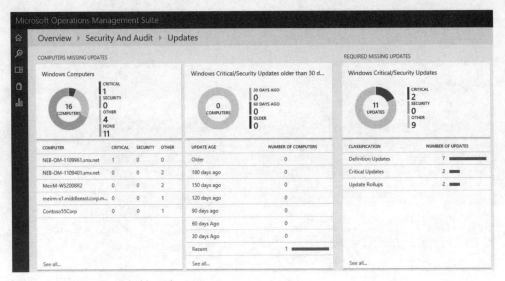

FIGURE 9-11 The Updates dashboard

From the three sections of this dashboard, you can quickly identify which computers are missing critical, security-related, or other types of updates. It also helps you identify how old the update is and which computers are missing it. These three views show the same information differently, which helps you assess your environment from different perspectives.

During an investigation process, you might need to cross-reference information; for example, say you identified that some systems are missing a critical update and now you want to understand if there are security events in these systems. You can use the Computers tile to search for the specific system or to obtain a list of the systems where security events were triggered. If you select this tile, a dashboard similar to the one in Figure 9-12 is displayed.

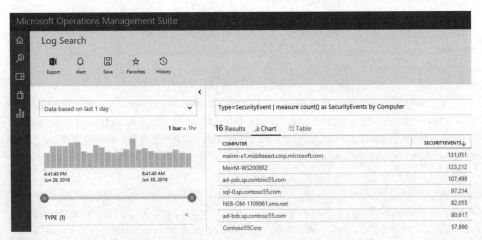

FIGURE 9-12 Searching for a security-related event

The Log Search dashboard in OMS inherits the Log Analytics search feature[4], which you can use to combine and correlate any machine data from multiple sources within your environment. As you select each computer on the right, the details of the security events that were trigged are displayed, as shown in Figure 9-13.

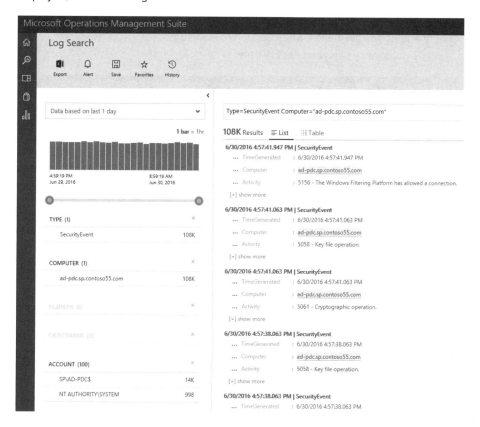

FIGURE 9-13 Filtering the search results for one computer

Figure 9-13 shows an example of the result when you select a computer that has many security events. The advantage of this view is that you can quickly identify the type of event and the activity that was performed. This valuable piece of information can be used during a security investigation process.

---

[4] For more information about search syntax, read the article "Log Analytics search reference" at *https://azure.microsoft.com/documentation/articles/log-analytics-search-reference*.

Identity and access control

As stated in Chapter 2, "Identity protection in Azure," 95 percent of data breach incidents involve some sort of credential theft; therefore, it is imperative that you closely monitor your identity and access across devices and locations. In a hybrid environment with resources located in multiple clouds and on-premises, this becomes even more critical. To help with monitoring, you can use the Identity And Access tile in the OMS Security And Audit dashboard. Figure 9-14 shows an example of what's displayed when you select this tile.

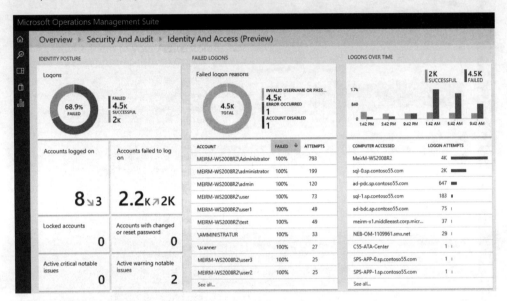

FIGURE 9-14 Identity And Access dashboard

The tiles on this dashboard help you to identify failed and successful logon attempts and the reason that some logons were not successful. The dashboard also provides a comprehensive timeline of successful and failed logon attempts. Other tiles, located under the Identity Posture section, can help you to identify the number of:

- Accounts that were logged on
- Accounts that failed to log on
- Locked accounts
- Accounts with a changed or reset password
- Active critical issues
- Active warning issues

If you want to further investigate any of those attributes, you can select the tile to open another dashboard that displays more details based on a search result, similar to what was shown in Figure 9-12.

Alerts and threats

OMS Security and Audit has a dedicated section to address what it calls *notable issues*[5], which are basically security alerts ranked by criticality, as shown in Figure 9-15.

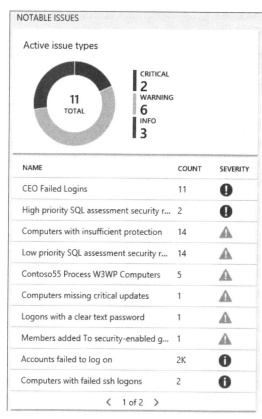

FIGURE 9-15 Current list of notable issues

[5] For more information about notable issues, read the article "OMS security notable issues" at
  https://blogs.technet.microsoft.com/msoms/2016/05/31/oms-security-notable-issues.

You can use the diagram shown in Figure 9-15 to access the active issues based on the criticality. The information under it provides a brief description of the active issue, the number of occurrences of that issue, and the severity. If you select one of these issues, another dashboard with more details about that problem appears, as shown in Figure 9-16.

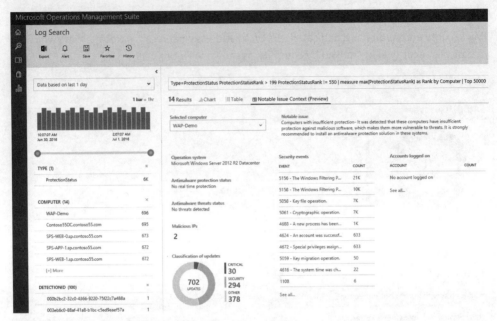

FIGURE 9-16 Details of a specific notable issue

This dashboard provides useful information for security administrators who are trying to understand how this issue affects this particular system. On the right is the full explanation of the notable issue, the security events that are associated with it, and the antimalware status for this system. With this information, you can understand the impact of the issue on the target system, and also what needs to be done to resolve it.

You can use this information in a variety of scenarios, such as incident response, forensics investigation, or post-mortem analysis. However, in some circumstances, you might not see any evidence that the target system was compromised, which could lead you to believe that the system is secure. If a system doesn't raise an alert, it might mean that it's being used by a compromised network to perform illicit activity. To identify potential issues on outgoing and incoming activity, you can use the information available in the Threat Intelligence[6] section, as shown in Figure 9-17.

---

[6] For more information about this capability, read the article "Monitoring and responding to security alerts in Operations Management Suite Security and Audit Solution" at *https://azure.microsoft.com/documentation /articles/oms-security-responding-alerts*.

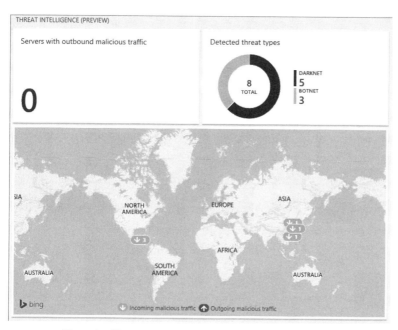

FIGURE 9-17 Threat Intelligence section

By using this option, security administrators can identify security threats against the environment; for example, they could identify whether a particular computer is part of a botnet. Computers can become nodes in a botnet when attackers illicitly install malware that secretly connects this computer to the command and control. It can also identify potential threats coming from underground communication channels, such as darknet. To build this threat intelligence, OMS Security and Audit uses data coming from multiple sources within Microsoft. OMS Security and Audit uses this data to identify potential threats against your environment. In hybrid environments, OMS will detect if there are computers inside the network (on-premises or in the cloud) that are communicating with a botnet located outside the network.

## CHAPTER 10

Operations and management in the cloud

After you correctly configure all your resources to use the Microsoft Azure security capabilities, you should ensure that your operations are also employing security considerations in all management phases. Throughout this book, you learned how Azure can help protect your cloud resources by using built-in capabilities. This chapter provides a scenario in which the target company needs to design its cloud infrastructure, taking into consideration connectivity with on-premises resources, virtual machine (VM) protection, and secure operations.

This chapter explains how to combine the capabilities that were described throughout this book to accomplish this fictitious organization's goals.

Scenario

Many people struggle to understand the difference between on-premises computing and cloud computing. Most of you have many years of experience with on-premises computing, and with that, on-premises security. You have your technologies, processes, and procedures in place, and those have all withstood the test of time.

But now you're confronted with moving to the cloud. How do you learn about cloud computing? How can you use what you understand about on-premises computing and apply that knowledge to cloud computing?

The following scenario might help you understand cloud computing security. The scenario begins with a fictitious company named Contoso. Contoso is a multinational company and has a complex network that includes approximately 25,000 users. The company's computing and network infrastructure has been in place for more than 15 years. It has well-established security controls in place for compute, networking, and storage.

The chief technical officer has given the Contoso IT organization a directive to begin moving corporate assets to the cloud. This directive is driven by the fact that the company no longer wants to invest in expanding your on-premises datacenters. The Contoso datacenters are nearing maximum capacity. Any more compute, storage, or networking expansion must be done with a public cloud service provider.

The Contoso IT administrators have always been careful in evaluating new solutions. Due to the nature of the business, the company cannot risk extended periods of downtime due to untested solutions. For this reason, they have decided to begin with a small pilot project that will result in extending the company's on-premises datacenter into the Azure public cloud.

The IT administrators first decide which cloud service model to use. They know about infrastructure as a service (IaaS), platform as a service (PaaS), and software as a service (SaaS). Given that the motive for moving to the cloud is to stop the rising costs of on-premises datacenters, they decide that the best place for them to start is with IaaS. They understand the benefits of PaaS and SaaS, and will consider those cloud service models in the future.

If possible, Contoso would like to mirror components of its infrastructure in Azure IaaS. Its current infrastructure provides, at a high level, the following:

- A Class A private address network that has multiple subnets
- Network access control devices located between subnets
- Firewalls and proxies used for all Internet connectivity, inbound and outbound
- Multiple perimeter networks in place at the Internet edges
- Dedicated storage arrays used to support file services and database servers
- Widespread use of virtualization, mostly Hyper-V, but with islands of VMware and Citrix
- Active Directory–integrated DHCP service
- Active Directory–integrated authentication for the company's applications
- Microsoft Antimalware on all client systems, and non–Microsoft antimalware on servers
- Multitier applications

Given that this is the company's current design, what can the Contoso IT administrators do to instantiate a similar design in Azure?

Design considerations

The IT administrators need to consider the following design issues when extending their on-premises infrastructure into Azure IaaS.

- How will they connect their on-premises infrastructure to Azure Virtual Networks?
- How will they handle IP addressing?
- How is subnetting done in Azure?
- How is network access control done between subnets?
- How is inbound and outbound Internet access controlled on Azure Virtual Networks?
- How is storage deployed and managed in Azure?
- How do they map their current VM sizes to the sizes available in Azure?

- How do they deploy multitier applications in Azure?
- How do they improve security and perform incident response in Azure?
- How do they integrate their on-premises identity infrastructure with Azure?
- How do they protect their VMs from viruses and other types of malware?

The IT administrators asked all these questions and performed their due-diligence research. After reviewing their options, they decided on the following for the initial design for their pilot project:

- The goal of the pilot project is to show that they can effectively extend their on-premises infrastructure into Azure.
- They will use a site-to-site VPN for the initial phases of the project. Subsequent project phases will use Azure ExpressRoute so that the IT administrators have the bandwidth needed to deploy multiple applications in Azure IaaS.
- On-premises subnets are defined by the roles of the servers on those subnets. The IT administrators will do the same in Azure, by using a Class C private address space, and creating a subnet so that they can add more Azure Virtual Networks in the future. They are also careful not to overlap their address spaces between on-premises and Azure.
- Network access control between subnets will initially be performed by Network Security Groups (NSGs). In the future, the IT administrators will investigate using virtual network appliances, which will give them an additional level of security.
- Inbound and outbound access from and to the Internet will be controlled by NSGs. In addition, the administrators will configure forced tunneling so that VMs on Azure Virtual Networks are not able to initiate outbound connections to the Internet but can respond to inbound requests.
- Azure Storage will be used to support databases and file services.
- The IT administrators will map on-premises VM sizes to those available in Azure. They will also standardize VM sizes to simplify the deployment.
- Multitier applications will be deployed by placing each tier on different subnets and by creating NSG rules to apply to all VMs in each subnet. This will simplify network access control management.
- Incident response will use Azure Security Center.
- Microsoft Antimalware will be installed on all VMs.
- They will extend their on-premises Active Directory deployment into Azure so that they do not need to change their authentication scheme.
- They will integrate Azure Active Directory (Azure AD) with their on-premises Active Directory so that they can use their on-premises credentials to manage their infrastructure through the Azure portal.

Figure 10-1 provides a general view of the structure of the pilot project.

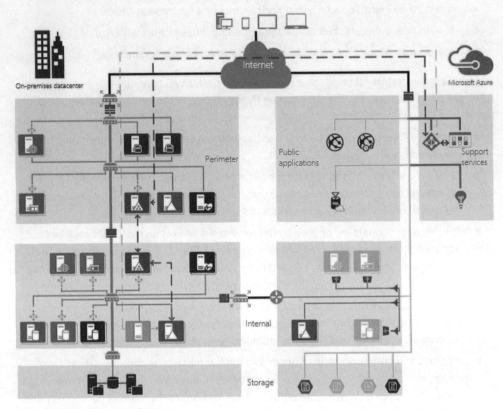

FIGURE 10-1 The Contoso pilot project

Now that you have an understanding of the company's goals and design decisions, you need to know how to use Azure Security Center to support your security operations and incident response. The next section explains how Azure Security Center can be a powerful and effective partner in helping to secure your Azure deployments.

Azure Security Center for operations

After the Contoso IT administrators properly configure the environment based on the previously established design considerations, they need to maintain more secure operations for their resources located in Azure. The onboarding process in Security Center takes place by ensuring that all VMs have the Security Center agent installed. This process happens automatically when they enable data collection.

Operations security

The last thing any blue team member, incident handler, monitoring analyst, or forensic investigator wants to hear is, "Logs? What logs? We don't have any logs." As you consider adopting or expanding your use of Azure cloud services, be sure to consider the need for more secure management of those resources. There are very clear methods for avoiding the "What logs?" scenario, as provided by Azure Security Center. From your Azure portal, you have immediate access to these tools.

Azure Security Center helps you set security policies for your deployments, implement security recommendations to ensure best practices are adhered to, and monitor the security health of your assets, in addition to the partner solutions you might be using.

If you need detection and response, you can enable the robust options in Azure Security Center to manage security alerts. You can enable alerts for brute-force attempts via network and endpoint. You might want to know when your VMs are communicating with malicious IP addresses, or worse, when those same VMs show signs of being compromised.

Above all else, remember to enable, and leave enabled, Azure Security Center data collection. With data collection ensuring that you have an audit trail, and activity history, the Azure Monitoring Agent and the Azure Security Monitoring extension will scan for security-relevant data to send to Event Tracing for Windows (ETW). The Azure Monitoring Agent also reads your operating system event logs; ETW traces and writes the logs to the storage account you enable, along with security policies. The Monitoring Agent even includes crash dumps for in-depth analysis.

Azure Security Center gives you a convenient and centralized feature set that you can use to help protect, detect, and respond to your Azure deployments. No more "We don't have those logs." Feel empowered to conduct insightful root cause analysis and be able to instead say, "We prevented that attack and understand our adversary's behavior." The only thing you'll hear thereafter will be "Job well done."

Russ McRee
Principal Security PM Manager, Windows & Devices Group

After the IT administrators complete the onboarding process, they should focus on following the recommendations explained in Chapter 7, "Azure resource management security." After they apply all recommendations and the environment is stable, then the ongoing secure management takes place. Most of the operations management will be done by reviewing the information in the Prevention section of the Security Center dashboard, shown in Figure 10-2.

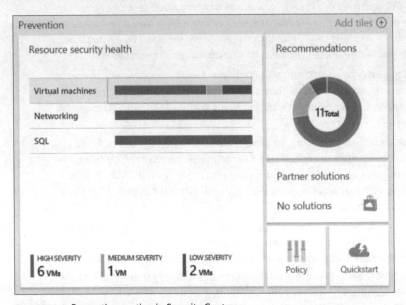

FIGURE 10-2 Prevention section in Security Center

As part of your operations process, be sure to review the resource security health of your Azure assets from this dashboard at least once a day. Ideally, you should have a dashboard without high and medium severity recommendations. However, depending on your environment size and type of business, this might not be possible, for example, if you have multiple tenants that are constantly provisioning new resources, such as Azure SQL Database servers and VMs. In this case, it is expected that as new resources are being provisioned, they will not automatically follow the baseline[1] recommendations.

Azure Security Center for incident response

Different organizations have different needs when the subject is incident response. For this reason, the incident response lifecycle used as a foundation for this section is based on the Microsoft five-stage[2] incident response process shown in Figure 10-3.

---

[1] Azure Security Center uses CCE (Common Configuration Enumeration) to assign unique identifiers for configuration rules. You can download these rules from *https://gallery.technet.microsoft.com/Azure-Security-Center-a789e335*.

[2] For more information about Incident Response in the Cloud, read the article "Microsoft Azure Security Response in the Cloud" at *https://gallery.technet.microsoft.com/Azure-Security-Response-in-dd18c678*.

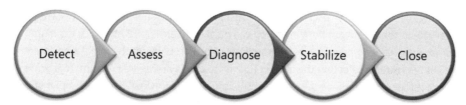

FIGURE 10-3 Incident response lifecycle used by Microsoft

The five lifecycle stages are briefly described here:

- **Detect**   Identification of a suspicious activity
- **Assess**   Triage of the identified suspicious activity
- **Diagnose**   Examination of the collected data to gain a better understanding of the issue
- **Stabilize**   Correction and repair of the services affected by the identified activity
- **Close**   The final phase, which is responsible for post-mortem analysis, technical documentation, final reporting, and incident closure

Now that you know the goal of each phase, you should understand how Security Center can be included to assist you during an incident response. You can use Security Center in multiple stages of an incident response lifecycle. For the first stage (Detect), you can use the Security Alerts tile, shown in Figure 10-4.

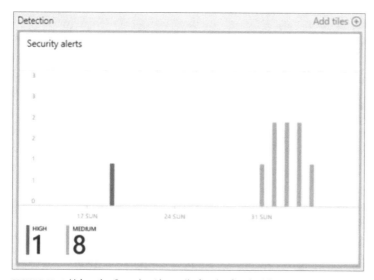

FIGURE 10-4 Using the Security Alerts tile for the first incident response stage

The Security Alerts tile can be used to detect a suspicious activity. Because Security Center automatically ranks the severity of the threat, you can quickly determine whether this is a high-priority threat that needs to be addressed immediately. You can perform the initial assessment (stage two) of the issue by selecting the alert in this tile to display more information regarding the issue. Select the resource that suffered the suspicious activity to view a detailed explanation of what happened, as shown in Figure 10-5.

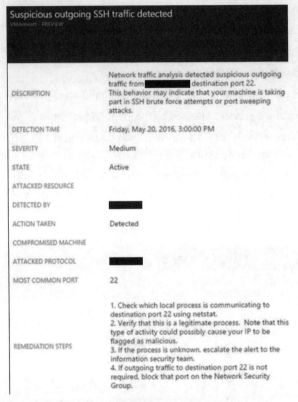

FIGURE 10-5 Complete details of the suspicious activity

This blade has a detailed explanation of the suspicious activity. You can better understand the behavior by reading the information in the Description field. You can review the Attacked Resource and Compromised Machine information also (which in this case are hidden for privacy reasons). The next section of this blade (which you can use for the third stage) is Remediation Steps. Security Center provides a comprehensive list of steps that you can use to remediate the issue. You can incorporate these suggestions as part of the resolution of the problem. Notice that these suggestions are not automatically run by Security Center. You should manually follow the steps and run them on the target system.

Azure Security Center for forensics investigation

Another process that is becoming very common nowadays is for organizations to have their own Forensics Team, and in many circumstances, this team is responsible for performing forensics analysis on the organizations' on-premises and cloud resources. For on-premises resources, forensics is not a new field, but forensics in the cloud might introduce some challenges depending on the type of service and the cloud provider. The scope of this section focuses only on how to use Security Center to assist you during a forensics investigation for your VMs located in the cloud[3].

Based on the information in "Guide to Integrating Forensic Techniques into Incident Response" from the National Institute of Standards and Technology (NIST)[4], forensics is about obtaining data from multiple sources to reconstruct an event and use this data as evidence for a case. Most of the work that can be done in Security Center to help in a forensics investigation is focused on data collection.

Part of the data collection process is a matter of answering questions regarding the issue that you are trying to investigate. For example, you can use Security Center to answer the following questions:

- When did the issue take place?
    - Use the Security Alert timeline to obtain this answer.
- What systems were affected?
    - Use the Security Alert tile to obtain the list of affected resources.
- What protocol and port were used to perform this attack?
    - Use the Security Alert blade with the details of the issue to obtain this answer.
- How many times did this attack take place?
    - Use the Security Alert timeline to obtain this answer.
- Did the attacker exploit any known vulnerability?
    - Use the Security Alert blade with the details of the issue to obtain this answer.
- Was the target computer fully updated?
    - Use the Resource Security Health tile for the VM in question to obtain this answer.

Answering questions like these is imperative during a forensics investigation process. The intent is to narrow as much as you can so your scope of action can be more focused, which makes it easier to reconstruct the event and rationalize the potential causes for the issue.

---

[3] Microsoft can work with customers to help them in performing forensic analysis of large scale breaches. For more information, read the article "Cloud Security as a Shared Responsibility" at *https://blogs.msdn.microsoft.com /azuresecurity/2015/06/05/cloud-security-as-a-shared-responsibility*.

[4] You can download the "Guide to Integrating Forensic Techniques into Incident Response" from *http://csrc.nist.gov /publications/nistpubs/800-86/SP800-86.pdf*.

Index

About the authors

YURI DIOGENES is a Senior Content Developer on the CSI Enterprise Mobility and Security Team, focusing on enterprise mobility solutions, Azure Security Center, and OMS Security. Previously, Yuri worked at Microsoft as a writer for the Windows Security team and as a Support Escalation Engineer for the CSS Forefront team. He has a Master of Science degree in Cybersecurity Intelligence and Forensics from Utica College and an MBA from FGF in Brazil, and he holds several industry certifications. He is co-author of *Enterprise Mobility Suite—Managing BYOD and Company-Owned Devices* (Microsoft Press, 2015), *Microsoft Forefront Threat Management Gateway (TMG) Administrator's Companion* (Microsoft Press, 2010), and three other Forefront titles from Microsoft Press.

DR. THOMAS SHINDER is a program manager in Azure Security Engineering and a 20-year veteran in IT security. Tom is best known for his work with ISA Server and TMG, publishing nine books on those topics. He was also the leading voice at *ISAserver.org*. After joining Microsoft in 2009, Tom spent time on the UAG DirectAccess team and then took a 3-year vacation from security to be a cloud infrastructure specialist and architect. He's now back where he belongs in security, and spends a good deal of time hugging his Azure Security Center console and hiding his secrets in Azure Key Vault.

DEBRA LITTLEJOHN SHINDER, MCSE, is a former police officer and police academy instructor who is self-employed as a technology consultant, trainer, and writer, specializing in network and cloud security. She has authored a number of books, including *Scene of the Cybercrime: Computer Forensics Handbook* (Syngress Publishing, 2002) and *Computer Networking Essentials* (Cisco Press, 2001). She has co-authored more than 20 additional books and worked as a tech editor, developmental editor, and contributor to more than 15 books. Deb is a lead author for *WindowSecurity.com* and *WindowsNetworking.com*, and a long-time contributor to the GFI Software blog and other technology publications, with more than 1,500 published articles in print magazines and on websites. Deb focuses on Microsoft products, and has been awarded the Microsoft MVP (Most Valuable Professional) award in the field of enterprise security for 14 years in a row. She lives and works in the Dallas-Fort Worth area and has taught law enforcement, computer networking, and security courses at Eastfield College in Mesquite, Texas. She currently sits on the advisory board of the Eastfield Criminal Justice Training Center Police Academy.

From technical overviews to drilldowns on special topics, get *free* ebooks from Microsoft Press at:

www.microsoftvirtualacademy.com/ebooks

Download your free ebooks in PDF, EPUB, and/or Mobi for Kindle formats.

Look for other great resources at Microsoft Virtual Academy, where you can learn new skills and help advance your career with free Microsoft training delivered by experts.

Microsoft Press

Now that you've read the book...

Tell us what you think!

Was it useful?
Did it teach you what you wanted to learn?
Was there room for improvement?

Let us know at http://aka.ms/tellpress

Your feedback goes directly to the staff at Microsoft Press,
and we read every one of your responses. Thanks in advance!